THE CHALLENGES OF JUDICIAL REFORM IN HAITI

JEAN SÉNAT FLEURY

Translated and Edited by Tom Luce and
Peter Luce, J.D. 2008, Tulane Law School
© 2009 All rights reserved, Hurah, Inc.
president@hurah-inc.org
http://www.hurah-inc.org

Rights to English Translation granted to:
Human Rights Accompaniment In Haiti – Hurah, Inc.
Tom Luce, President
by Jean Sénat Fleury, 2008
Cover designed by Gary Menuau
Photo Back cover: Tom Luce Delmas 32 – 04.05.09
Publisher: www.Lulu.com/content/7338897

ISBN: 978-0-557-21062-6

French Version Published in the United States
Steve Glines, Publisher
ISCS Press
145 Foster Street
Littleton, MA 01460
Cover designed by Gary Menuau
www.lulu.com/content/1106026

Photos: Joanna Gleason

Copyright French version: November 2007
National Library of Haiti
Jean Sénat Fleury

TABLE OF CONTENTS

DEDICATION 5

AUTHOR'S NOTE 6

FOREWORD 7

U.S. – HAITIAN PARTNERSHIP: HURAH, INC. - AUMOHD 8

INTRODUCTION 9
Distrusted and Inaccessible 9
Formal and Informal Law: Double Standards 9
Non-Existent Citizen Identification Mechanisms 10
Language Barriers 10
Private and Public Justice 10
Numerous Reform Proposals 11
Reform of the Haitian State 14
Balance of Power: An Independent Judiciary 14
Salaries and Other Benefits 15
Job Security 16
The Rule of Law 16
Justice for the Impoverished Majority 16

CHAPTER I: JUDICIAL INDEPENDENCE AND ACCESS TO
JUSTICE 19
STAKEHOLDERS IN THE JUDICIAL SYSTEM 20
Citizens 21
Police 21
Lawyers 21
Magistrates 23
District Court Magistrates 23
Dysfunction in the Prosecutor's Office and Courts of Minor Offense (Police
Courts) 23
Criminal Judges 24
The Investigative Office 25
SLOW JUSTICE AT EVERY LEVEL 26
The Penal Level 26
Political Interference 27
The Ministry of Justice 33
JUSTICE AND CORRUPTION 35
The Phenomenon of Corruption in Haiti 37
Corruption Among Magistrates 38
Rooting Out Corruption 38
Creation of A National Anti-Corruption Watchdog Group 41
Introduction of a Transparent Inspection System 42

Conduct a Massive Media Campaign 42
Respect for the Code of Ethics 42

CHAPTER II: REFORMING JUSTICE **44**

INSTITUTIONAL INDEPENDENCE OF JUDGES 47
TRAINING AND COMPETENCY 47
JUDICIAL INDEPENDENCE AND AUTONOMY 50
ADEQUATE PAY FOR MAGISTRATES 52
ACCESS TO JUSTICE FOR ALL 52
  Accessibility 53
  Hospitality 54
  Satisfaction 55
THE PRINCIPLE OF ACCESS TO RIGHTS 56
THE RIGHT TO A FAIR TRIAL 56
THE PRINCIPLE OF EXEMPTION FROM PAYMENT 56

CHAPTER III: RECOMMENDATIONS FOR JUDICIAL REFORM IN HAITI **60**

ESTABLISHING EFFECTIVE JUDICIAL INDEPENDENCE 60
  1. Short-Term Reforms 60
  2. Medium-Term Reforms 62
  3. Long-Term Reforms 65
LEGAL GUARANTEES FOR DEFENDANTS 66
  1. Short-Term Reforms 66
  2. Medium-term reforms 66
  3. Long-Term Reforms 67
REINFORCING THE RULE OF LAW 70
  1. Ensuring Public Safety: 71
  2. Ensuring Justice 71
  3. The Problem of Lawlessness 73
  4. Proposals for Eliminating Lawlessness 74
  5. Police Reform 74
  6. Human Rights 76
JUSTICE AND HUMAN RIGHTS 77
JUDICIAL REFORM BEGINS WITH ESTABLISHING THE RULE OF LAW 81

CHAPTER IV: JUDICIAL REFORM IN HAITI: A CHALLENGE TO BE OVERCOME **83**

REFLECTIONS FROM COLLEAGUES **88**

THE AUTHOR **121**

BIBLIOGRAPHY **122**

INDEX **125**

DEDICATION

This book is dedicated to all victims of the drifting tides of the Haitian judicial system, both silent and outspoken, to the thousands of compatriots discouraged from obtaining their rights by countless obstacles, whether from the judicial system's slowness and complexity, a lack of time or money, or simply out of fear of disturbing the status quo.

I also dedicate this work to Prosecutor Laraque Exantus, my classmate at the Faculty and co-worker in the Prosecutor's office, who was kidnapped from his home in February 1994 and who has been missing ever since.

    - Jean Sénat Fleury (French edition)

The English version of Judge Fleury's book is dedicated to the countless poor, unknown victims of abuses by both government (national and international) and politically motivated forces in Cité Soleil, Simon Pele, Gran Ravin, Croix-des-Bouquets and Plateau Centrale who have been at least given some basic assistance by our partner, AUMOHD. These victims, massacred and/or deprived of their homes through arson, illegally detained and beaten, can only achieve the justice detailed in this book when the reforms are implemented for their descendants. All proceeds of the sale of this book will go to support the real reform of justice through the work of AUMOHD and their Community Human Rights Councils. See our website: http://www.hurah-inc.org for updates and ways to contribute.

    - Tom Luce, President, Hurah, Inc. July 30, 2009

AUTHOR'S NOTE

Many of the concepts in this work were first explored in the book The *Supreme Court And Judicial Reform in Haiti*.[1] Building on previous research, this new analysis on Judicial Reform gives a precise diagnosis of the dysfunctional character of the Haitian judicial apparatus, and makes a list of recommendations forming the foundation of, and setting guidelines for, the most important elements of the judicial reform process.

Publication of this document is intended to allow its readers to better understand the challenges presented, and to provide insight for citizens toward strengthening the democratic order in Haiti by means of authentic reform of the judicial system.

Jean Sénat Fleury, Boston, September 10, 2007

---

[1] First printed and published in France in March 2006, this book analyzed the problem of judicial reform in Haiti. The analysis began after the decree of December 9, 2005 by the Boniface/Latortue government, arbitrarily dismissing five Supreme Court judges and replacing them with five new judges sworn in at the National Palace.

FOREWORD

Upon reading the program of HURAH- Human Rights Accompaniment in Haiti, Inc. and after a long conversation with Tom Luce and Attorney Evel Fanfan, I give my support of this program that I think can be helpful for Human Rights in Haiti. I am already in touch with many friends, for example judges, lawyers, to ask them to support this program and to offer their competence to HURAH.

Jean Sénat Fleury

3 Aug 2008, Boston - Jean Sénat Fleury, former Haitian judge and Tom Luce, President of **HURAH**, a non-partisan human rights group, spoke with Evel Fanfan of **AUMOHD** in Port-au-Prince via SKYPE as they launched a $100,000 campaign to expand AUMOHD'S legal aid to its Community Human Rights Councils (CHRCs) for impoverished Haitians. In his book, Judge Fleury calls for massive reform of the corrupt Haitian judicial system, including a call for community based legal assistance programs. The AUMOHD CHRC model has been widely praised by Judge Fleury. See the HURAH website at: http://www.hurah-inc.org; e-mail: president@hurah-inc.org Judge Fleury is a respected lawyer, legal scholar, and writer. His book, *The Challenges of Judicial Reform In Haiti,* is available at http://www.lulu.com /content/7338897.

U.S. – HAITIAN PARTNERSHIP: HURAH, INC. - AUMOHD

Human Rights Accompaniment In Haiti-Hurah, Inc. is a Vermont registered, 501(c)(3) charitable, educational agency. Tom Luce, President of **Hurah, Inc.** (left) and Attorney Evel Fanfan, President of **AUMOHD**, (right) met by chance at the Haitian National Penitentiary in April 2004. Mr. Luce was in Haiti with EPICA (Ecumenical Program In Central America And The Caribbean) on an investigative tour following the ouster of then-President Jean-Bertrand Aristide.

While visiting Prime Minister Yvon Neptune, jailed by the Latortue government, Mr. Luce met Mr. Fanfan, who was visiting a prisoner. Mr. Fanfan explained that he was part of a young professional, non-violent, non-partisan Haitian human rights group working with illegally imprisoned indigent clients.

Since first befriending a Haitian classmate during his years studying in Rome, Mr. Luce has followed the dream of liberating the poor and marginalized in underdeveloped countries. Mr. Fanfan invited Mr. Luce to return to Haiti to work with AUMOHD. Since then, HURAH has provided accompaniment and financial aid, while AUMOHD continues to work directly with illegally jailed prisoners. AUMOHD has created a unique model of service delivery, the *Community Human Rights Council* (CHRC). Victims and their families, community, school, church and civic leaders have formed non-violent, non-partisan CHRCs in four Haitian metropolitan areas to educate others about their legal rights and to advocate for the rights of those in their communities.

INTRODUCTION

Due to the lamentable state of the Haitian judicial system, obtaining justice is an extremely difficult proposition. A dearth of courts, low wages for court employees, frequent interference from the executive branch, a lack of proper education and legal training, fragile and infrequently applied laws - all of these factors contribute to a judicial system that is not trusted by the Haitian people, that does not achieve its stated purposes, and that does not fulfill its obligations to society.

Distrusted and Inaccessible

Today, nearly three quarters of Haiti's citizens live literally beyond the reach of the judicial system. This exclusion is true for rural areas as well as for sprawling urban areas that have resulted from rural migration. Rural areas are almost completely devoid of any security services; police force units are stationed exclusively in the mid-sized and small urban areas. Indeed, no judicial apparatus whatsoever currently exists at the level of the most basic Haitian territorial subdivision, the *commune* (the smallest administrative district governed by a mayor and a council). Meanwhile, for the majority of Haiti's citizens the essential routines of daily life are played out at this level. Paradoxically, people who migrate from rural areas to the city face the same access problem, jammed into huge zones with poor housing and without any access to legal services. Such close proximity usually works in favor of urban populations in terms of more effective access to the judicial system, but not in Haiti.

Formal and Informal Law: Double Standards

De facto control of these two great swaths of the Haitian populace – the rural and urban masses – is primarily achieved through application of informal laws governing matrimonial relations (common law marriage), the exercise of property rights, and the levying of property taxes (both rural and urban). These non-codified laws often conflict with official law based on the Napoleonic Code, which follows a fundamentally different logic. In fact, Haiti is a country with two different judicial orders. This dual system would not pose a problem if Haiti were recognized as a juridically plural state. However, the official judicial system does not recognize the existence of common or informal law. The informal system is officially ignored and, with it, so are most of the Haitian people, who continue to govern their social functions according to a double set of legal standards.

Non-Existent Citizen Identification Mechanisms

In Haiti, the government has neglected the basic task of identifying its citizens. An Inter-American Development Bank (IDB) report estimated that 40% of Haiti's citizenry is undocumented, and therefore, completely outside the legal system. In the backcountry, traditionally, any citizenship identification service worthy of the name is non-functional. This is akin to the situation described by Victor Schoelcher in 1843 in the language of the time: "In the midst of the immense administrative disorder of this country, where all forms borrowed from civilization are for show, there is not even any formal citizenship, and outside the cities, you die and you are buried without anyone knowing it except your neighbors." Most of the country is thus left in a state of permanent civic anonymity, which prevents citizens from benefiting from even the most minimal prerogatives attached to all individuals through the mere fact of one's existence – the individual rights of personhood, to one's name, to citizenship, to one's legal capacity, and the right to establish a domicile.

Language Barriers

The entire apparatus of formal justice in Haiti effectively rests both on the use of the written word and on the French language, even though 60% of the population is illiterate, and fewer than 10% speak French fluently. At every level of society, the dualities of spoken Creole and written French - in a country where less than 10% of the population speaks French at all - drastically reduces the effectiveness and clarity of the judicial function.

Private and Public Justice

Because justice is a public service, access to it must be guaranteed to all, without prejudice. Access to justice can be measured in terms of the geographical location of courts, the distance that must be traveled to reach them, the cost of available services, and the language in which judicial decisions are rendered. The number of citizens to whom justice is accessible is sharply reduced when the geographic location of courts across Haiti today is taken into account, a fact further demonstrated by the per capita distribution of courts in Haiti and by the number of judges currently serving in them. As a result, Haitians have resorted to implementing **"private justice."** In practice, victims of serious violations of their fundamental liberties more often than not choose private justice rather than pursuing legal avenues of obtaining redress. The temptation to make one's own justice is a direct result of this lack of access. From the perspective of victims of offenses, this vengeance-based approach is faster, has more direct effect, and is more stable. It is as if the era of the ancient law of retaliation *(La Loi du Talion*, or "eye for an eye*)* had never ended in Haiti.

Numerous Reform Proposals

The performance of the Haitian judicial system has been the subject of numerous evaluations, diagnoses, studies, analyses and reports, both by international and national experts. These specialists have each proposed short-, mid- and long-term action plans to either completely reform the system, or to improve its performance.[2]

---

[2] In March 2006 The Government of Canada and the United Nations Development Program (UNDP) began collaborating in support for Haitian judicial reform. The program is intended to encourage activity in the area of institutional support, strengthening the penal code, the prison system, legislative reforms, and judicial training. Financed for an initial period of three years, the program has a total budget estimated at US $ 11.6 million, and for the moment is covered up to $5.655.000USD ($5.000.000CA Canadian dollars and $1.500.000US from the UNDP). The Government and donor countries should b e congratulated for agreeing on the need for reforming the Haitian judicial system. However it must be noted most of the numerous initiatives in this field have not improved the justice system's operations. In addition to concrete needs regarding financing, training and evaluation, even greater coherence and coordination between MINUSTAH and the HAITIAN STATE is required so that reform can give rise to a strong, independent judicial system, ready to defend basic rights and to protect the most vulnerable.

It is always important not to reproduce the errors of the past. Any cooperative reform program must integrate from the outset provisions that make it possible to fight politicization, corruption, bad management and charges of human rights violations that have characterized the judiciary and the police force, and must bring those responsible to justice. In addition, reform of the judicial system, the police force and the prisons must be considered as interdependent and synchronized processes. Experience has shown that if training and aid provided to the police force did not have he desired result, it was due to the fact that the justice system and the police force did not advance according to the same rhythm.

The following requests can be made of the international community:

a) Commit to supporting Haiti in a lasting way by respecting commitments entered into by international donors to allocate to financial resources to achieve the objectives of eradicating poverty and infant mortality, providing basic education and proper care for the environment;

b) Help the country to work to become a State based on the Rule of Law and to help consolidate its institutions;

c) Redefine the deployment of MINUSTAH personnel by replacing a portion of military troops with technicians (engineers, doctors, agronomists, lawyers, police officers, economists, instructors etc.) to help to rebuild the country's basic infrastructure;

d) Make it so that MINUSTAH's redefined mandate is regularly renewed in order to bring about the necessary continuity required for the country's stabilization and so that efforts by the international community ensure a better future for Haitians. It is important to break the cycle of multiplication of short-term international missions to allow Haiti to develop a permanent solution to the crises that chronically overpower the country, whether financial or concerning human rights.

MINUSTAH's challenge with regard to institutional strengthening of the justice system is to define and unify an intervention strategy and a common method for the entire system, by moving beyond the emergency measures that have characterized existing approaches and providing a single point of control for overall strategy – giving priority to institutional development. For that, we think that that the UNDP should facilitate strategic planning, coordination, follow-up and evaluation of activities as well as the implementation of support activities.

Whatever United Nations body is charged with carrying out a particular project (UNDP, MINUSTAH, UNICEF, UNESCO, FAO), the installation of an institutional support plan must obey a single and central objective. This will make it possible to avoid implementing different methods within the same system, and to give the plan an internal coherence and increased effectiveness. The strategic approach gives a unified direction to the various projects. Finally, this same approach should as a whole relate to the justice system while

Summarizing all of the notable efforts of these individuals is beyond the scope of this book, however, several studies deserve mention here. In particular, the studies of the International Civil Mission in Haiti (MICIVIH), notably *The Judicial system in Haiti – Analysis of Penal Aspects and Penal Procedures*; the periodic reports of the General Secretary of the United Nations on the activities of MICIVIH in 1998, and the Mission of the Civil Police Force of the United Nations in Haiti (MIPONUH), as well as the reports of Mr. Adama Dieng, independent expert of the Human Rights Commission and his colleague, Louis Joinet. The detailed evaluations of Haitian courts carried out with American cooperation since 1995 - a study prepared for USAID in November 1997 titled *"Assessment of the Justice Sector in Haiti,"* a July 1998 evaluation of the programs managed by USAID, and the December 1997 European Union report - also deserve mention. Finally, the October 1999 Report of the Haitian Justice Commission, sponsored by the United Nations Development Program (UNDP), Office for Latin America and the Caribbean, broke important ground regarding the problems of justice in Haiti. This latter initiative was based on the expertise of various international legal organizations (Canada, Argentina, France) as well as on the expertise of Haitian professionals (lawyers, anthropologists, and human rights activists).

In Haiti, two commissions undertook judicial reform work on a major scale, namely the National Commission On Truth and Justice, whose 1995 report contains notable recommendations for the reform of judicial institutions, and the Preparatory Commission for The Reform of Rights and Justice (CPRDJ) (1997-1999) which produced, among several documents, a Document of General Policy, a Strategic Plan and a short-term Action Plan.

The one word repeated endlessly in all of these studies in connection with the notion of justice in Haiti, even at the highest levels, is **"failure."** Haitian and foreign specialists alike are unanimous in recognizing the dysfunction of the Haitian judicial apparatus. This official verdict, already outdated, for all practical purposes, is unanimous. The debate revolves only around the

---

integrating all its elements and avoiding "compartmentalization" (police force-justice-prison) among branches of the judiciary.

blueprint for reform. But the big question remains the order of the day: which system of justice is appropriate for Haiti?

Reform of the Haitian State

In order for reform of the Haitian judicial system to succeed, it is first of all necessary to consider reform of the Haitian State. It is difficult to conceive of the reform of justice without also reforming the State in its relationship with political structures and civil society.[3] The reform of justice implies serious transformations within the State and in civil society. One of the fundamental values on which the theory of the Rule of Law is based is respect for the law in the first place by all State authorities that, in their turn, are responsible for applying the law. Respect for the law indisputably comprises the fundamental theory on which a Democracy by Rule of Law is based.

Balance of Power: An Independent Judiciary

Judicial reform is inconceivable without also restoring the balance of powers, which is a corollary of the principle of the separation of powers consecrated in the 1987 Constitution. Implementation of judicial reforms is therefore a sizeable problem. Avoiding abuses of citizens' rights begins with respecting judicial standards. But judicial reform also includes protecting the judiciary's civil servants. All civil servants must be guaranteed effective police protection in the exercise of their duties. Some guarantees for members of the judiciary are therefore required: first, regarding recruitment, and what today we call stakeholder participation. This means, at the very least and in whatever form it takes, recognizing a magistrate's right not only to self-expression, but also the right to collaborate in the definition of the magistrate's mission, thereby contributing to the ennoblement of that mission,

---

[3] Undertaking justice reform in a country that is in the process of establishing the Rule of Law raises not just technical problems. In fact, it is a matter of constructing democracy itself. On the one hand, democracy is not only built by "political" men and women or by civil servants, but by all citizens, just as justice is not built, nor does it reform itself by the system's operators, but more by those who ultimately benefit from it. The reform process must thus be open and participatory. In addition, reform that is not supported by genuine internal reflection is doomed to fail from the outset.

and in some measure strengthening it, thus imbuing the magistrate's mission with an ethical or moral dimension.

Professional advancement is also a crucial matter, because once one recruits a civil servant, one cannot assume that such advancement will occur merely because of someone else's good will, or will not be obstructed by a system that lacks proper career development structures. Of course, beyond the career ladder, the right to adequate pension and retirement guarantees also poses significant problems.

As it currently functions, the judicial apparatus is unable to guarantee protection for civil servants in the performance of their duties. The judiciary is completely dependent upon the executive power under the Minister of Justice. Haiti's tradition of external authority over the judicial branch has only exacerbated this problem.

Salaries and Other Benefits

The level of wages and benefits offered to judicial magistrates is insignificant when compared to the importance of their work and to the risks they incur.[4] It is therefore understandable when fraud corrupts the system. The opportunities for corruption - of rendering decisions in exchange for bribes, promises of promotion or other forms of reward - appear enormous. But financial gain is not the only issue. The hope of making a career for oneself is also important. The advantages that stem from successful legal careers are extremely attractive, and are important for the health of any sound professional judiciary. Realistic and sufficient career advancement opportunities must exist in order to be able to attract

---

[4] The judge functions as a "a kind of pariah" (Jean Joseph Exumé) in Haitian society: if anyone can terrorize judges by threatening them or their families without fear of prosecution, if the judge's role is blatantly duplicated in practice by the Government Prosecutor, if judges can be removed at any time without explanation from political authorities, responsibility for the system's general bankruptcy cannot plausibly be imputed to the judiciary alone, nor is it safe to assume that mere training in the Napoleonic Code ought to suffice to solve the problem. At a time when the State itself suffers from a lack of authority from where will judges, who are the State's creation, draw theirs? In addition, it is essential to give magistrates the social status they deserve and fair salaries that correspond with their responsibilities and personal risks.

good lawyers to the system. In Haiti, no viable career paths exist for civil servants in the judiciary.

Job Security

From the perspective of job security, civil servants in the judiciary who feel their rights have been violated while performing their duties must have recourse to the services of a functioning administrative court. The jobs of judges who apply the law correctly, but who happen to dissatisfy their superiors or other authority figures, must not be threatened.[5] In reality, however, judges are "pariahs" in the Haitian judicial system, and can be fired without cause at any time by government officials.

The Rule of Law

Judicial reform is also related to the establishment of the Rule of Law. The Rule of Law implies taking into account the basic rights inherent in the human person: the rights to life, health, employment, food, education, housing and safety. These fundamental rights are ignored and ridiculed in Haiti, which is ranked last among countries in the Western hemisphere in protecting them.

Justice for the Impoverished Majority

Faced with these facts, there is no doubt that reform of the Haitian judicial system is a necessity.[6] But then the unanswered

---

[5] During the five last years, several Magistrates have denounced pressure from members of the executive branch at the local or central level. Some were relieved of their positions or were forced into exile for refusing to yield to this pressure.

[6] Long term reforms for national development of the Haitian judicial system are unrealistic, but urgent many short term provisions are essential, such as:

a) Stabilization of the socio-political situation beginning with a policy of national reconciliation, and a national dialogue that emphasizes construction of peace and development.

b) Search for consensus on a comprehensive list of fundamental questions such as universal education, fighting against poverty, environmental policies, reduction of inequality, social justice, the need for the Rule of Law. All this

question is this: is it feasible to attempt to engineer the development of a society of laws from the top down – by encouraging participation in the basic exercise of the prerogatives of citizenship, by promoting and defending fundamental rights such as the right to vote, without discounting a person's cultural heritage and imposing a worldview based solely on one's legal identity? Taking a hard look at the judicial system in place today, how can the Haitian people even conceive of equitable access to justice when 80% of them live below poverty line and when 60% are illiterate?[7] How can there be any lasting results from reform efforts, indeed, when the Haitian state and international donors continue to try to graft judicial frameworks conceived for and implemented by rich, developed countries onto Haiti, a poor nation, deprived of even the most basic elements of a national infrastructure?[8] After independence from France, the system of

---

with the objective of ensuring basic education for all, reducing poverty by reviving the economy and finally, ensuring a sustainable environment.

[7] According to data provided by the Ministry of Education's National Planning Agency, a total of 17,812 schools exist in Haiti. From this number, only 1,431 public schools are listed, or 8% of the total, which consists of 531,974 pupils or approximately 20% of the national total of 2,672,801 pupils. In other words, 92% of the country's schools educate only 44% of Haiti's students. (AHE: Conference on the economy of education, March 2005.)

[8] The Haitian population is reported to be approximately 8.5 million people, half of who are younger than 21 years of age; 60% currently live in rural areas. The population's annual growth rate has stabilized around 2.5%. Marked by economic and political instability that has lasted two decades, Haitian household standards of living have not improved since 1990. Indeed, 75% of Haiti's population earns an income of less than 100 Gourdes per day, equivalent to approximately $2.50 American dollars, whereas more than half of the country's citizens, approximately 4.5 million inhabitants live on less than 45 Gourdes per day, equivalent to approximately one American dollar.

From an average income of $500 dollars in 1990, the per capita GDP fell 28% in 1997; in 2003 the per capita GDP was at $382 dollars, or less than 67% of its 1990 level. These figures explain why daily per capita incomes fell dramatically from an average of $1.36 (American dollars) per day in 1990 to $0.90 cents (American) in 2003. Haiti is the poorest country in the Americas. Regards protection of basic human rights, Haiti ranks 150th out of 173 countries. Approximately 40% of homes lack adequate nourishment and 70% of the adult population is unemployed. Life expectancy at birth is lower than fifty years and infant mortality was 79 per thousand in 2002. Nearly two thirds of

civil and criminal law that was put in place was modeled on the French judicial tradition, the Napoleonic Code. However, Haitians - for the most part poor, illiterate, and superstitious - have never adapted to life under the aegis of a judicial regime that has repeatedly scorned all of their historic, cultural and customary traditions. Wouldn't it be better simply to say, in this case, that judicial reform in Haiti should involve envisioning another system of justice better adapted to Haiti's historical, cultural, social, and economic realities?[9]

---

the population lives below the national threshold of poverty. (UNDP, *Economic and Social Situation of Haiti in 2004*, PAP. August 2005.)

[9] This concept refers to the institutions responsible for distributing justice and reducing infractions of the law in Haiti - the justice system and the police force - that seem today completely overwhelmed vis-à-vis new problems. These institutions possess neither the judicial tools nor the manpower to enable them to face these new dangers. Two paths are then offered to Haiti:

a) The essential one, impossible to avoid: judicial reform. However, due to a lack of anthropological understanding of the nature of the judicial institution, the Haitian judiciary continues to lose credibility every day, and legal professionals are incapable of stopping this process.

b) The essential one, impossible to circumvent: the professionalization of the police force that has, in twelve years of existence, experienced problems of all kinds. One or the other of these reforms will come about through the training of a new generation of professionals capable of carrying out the reform project.

CHAPTER I:
JUDICIAL INDEPENDENCE AND
ACCESS TO JUSTICE

One of the principal conditions necessary to ensure access to justice is the existence of an independent judicial power. In Haiti, the judicial apparatus is in a state of serious crisis, and has failed to deliver justice in any meaningful way.[10] According to a report published by The Inter-American Commission on Human Rights (IACHR), "[t]he Haitian judicial system is like a market where everything can be bought and sold. One must pay to send someone to prison, and in the same way, one must have money to get someone out of prison."

This type of criticism – although perhaps exaggerated – is not unfounded if the influence of money on certain decisions rendered by Haitian courts and tribunals is taken into account. Indeed, the Haitian system, far from impartially dispensing justice, is often permissive and lax toward some but obstinate toward others, depending on the degree of societal influence of the party - politically rich or poor, well-educated or illiterate, gentleman or peasant. The result: administration of justice is weak, slow, partisan and highly dependent on circumstance.[11]

In its operation, the Haitian judicial system allows the worst

---

[10] The topic of judicial reform is not a new one. Not a single conference or symposium of journalist has failed to discuss the question of the dysfunctional character of the Haitian judicial system. Among Haitian society's numerous deficiencies, and in addition to dissatisfaction of defendants, judicial reform remains one of the most contentious issues, resulting in various protest movements led by legal professionals: lawyers, clerks, prison staff and, the fact is sufficiently rare to go unnoticed, even Haitian magistrates themselves united under ANAMAH (the National Association of Haitian Magistrates) have expressed complaints and have adhered to the concept of reform.

[11] Despite the concerns of the 1987 Constitution, the judicial branch in Haiti cannot be considered independent. The judiciary is almost entirely dependent on the executive power, a situation that grants almost complete control over the judiciary to the executive branch. The executive branch intervenes not only in the nomination of magistrates but also in their dismissal, which reinforces the authority of the executive branch over the judiciary.

iniquities of the country's entire social fabric to proliferate. In fact, the principle observation of those who direct their attention to the problems of Haiti's judiciary is that they come face-to-face with a completely dysfunctional system.[12]

STAKEHOLDERS IN THE JUDICIAL SYSTEM

All those who currently contribute to the formation and development of the judicial system in Haiti have failed in their roles.[13]

---

[12] The word "Justice" is not to be understood here in its original meaning, that is to say as an organized institution, or a body that brings together magistrates and support staff, but in its jurisdictional meaning, as used in the expression "to render justice", that is, to describe the search for a just solution. The word Justice is employed to indicate all institutions that allow justice to be rendered, i.e. simple cases between private individuals, or between private individuals and the State. The principle that any legal solution is subject to judicial review to ensure its legitimacy is important. This eventual potential oversight constitutes an essential guarantee for the respect of public and private freedoms. However, observers of the challenges posed by the Haitian judicial system are confronted rather with a system of generalized injustice.

[13] Few people today in Haiti dispute the need for establishing a coherent and effective system of justice and most go no further than stating that all the stakeholders who contribute to the formation of the functionality of the justice system are failing. Nevertheless, there are a certain number of obstacles, which in practice prevent implementation of a reform process for the Haitian judicial apparatus. How should we go about removing these obstacles? This is the objective of the long-term strategy proposed by the United Nations Development Program (UNDP) in a study carried out in October 1999 on justice in Haiti, and that takes into account of the fact that certain of these obstacles are more important and possess a strong deterrent power. For example, on the structural level, the societal duality and the permanent situation of conflict in which the protagonists find themselves. This kind of situation needs to be confronted by concrete measures that, without seeking to change the culture of an entire people – a practice of which many authoritarian solutions too often dream --would allow, on the contrary, an attempt at reconciling the situation, all the while rescuing it little by little from obstacles and the vicious circle/eternal dynamic of oppression/escape.

On the other hand, on the societal level, in a place where ingrained habits have not yet strongly taken root, analyzing the phenomenon of State and national weakness is recommended to encourage citizens to work together.

All this leads us to prioritize the fundamental needs of the country's active citizenry, not those of institutions, even if improved. The State that everyone is

Citizens

Citizens lack basic civic education and are ignorant of the rules of the judicial system. [14]

Police

Poorly equipped, badly trained, and poorly paid, the police officer plays the role of an extra on a movie set. He is simultaneously both an actor in, and victim of the system. [15]

Lawyers

Lawyers are professionals in the law, members of a bar, and come before the courts to defend their clients. If the legal profession contains qualified, competent and honest lawyers who are respectful of legal principles, there are also those who, insofar

---

waiting for will not be build upon passive and frightened subjects, but rather on agents from the entirety of civil society that alone will able to overcome today's obstacles.

To carry out the essential choices, the behaviors of a group of agents in the system were analyzed: the citizen, the police officer, lawyers, businessmen, notaries, land-surveyors, clerks, ushers, and magistrates. However, in making this behavioral study, we were conscious of not having taken into account all the actors implied in the system.

[14] The expression "civic education" is meant to include the State's obligation to contribute to training its people, its citizens. Civic education also means a broader, more practical vision of education. Within the framework of promoting the Rule of Law, civic education encourages citizens to participate in the government, one of the fundamental hallmarks of a democracy. Civic participation enables citizens to play the key role of in a democracy. Through civic education, citizens understand that they have not just the right but also a duty to participate in the country's decision-making process. In Haiti, the absence of civic education among its citizens is coupled with ignorance of the rules of the judicial system. The saying "ignorance of the law excuses no one," is only found in treatises. The Haitian State has made no efforts to educate people about their rights and civic obligations.

[15] Police officers' violent behavior arises from feeling abused by leaders who do not establish working conditions that allow policemen to perform their duties effectively and professionally.

as their practice is concerned, are so dysfunctional they generate a proportionate share of criminality and other dangerous social ills. In fact, many individuals with no academic training at all – who hold no more than a high school diploma - currently stand before the Courts of the Republic and plead cases as lawyers.[16] The acceptance of this practice over time has only served to legitimize this experiment in mediocrity.

A few lawyers have engaged in "shady practices" in order to make a name for themselves, and have monopolized the system to the detriment of a great number of their fellow members of the bar not powerful enough to manipulate the judicial system. Thanks to friendly judges they keep in their pockets or to accomplice clerks or court employees, these entrepreneurs, called "big-shot" lawyers, get satisfaction for their clients by obtaining "fake" default judgments containing trumped up, unlawful charges against adversaries. Often, these "big-shot" lawyers possess only a cursory knowledge of the law. Assisted by notaries, architects excelling in the manufacture of forged documents, these professionals very quickly dominate the scene.

The system is also crammed with individuals known as "proxies," who are also often simple "racketeers", operating outside all legal standards and sowing corruption and vice in the system.[17]

---

[16] The decree of March 29, 1979 regulates the profession of lawyer which is carried out within the framework of a co-operative organization called the Order of the Bar, which enjoys a legal identity and has the right to monitor and discipline its members. The decree provides that there be, in each Civil Court jurisdiction, an Order of Lawyers. Each Bar is autonomous.

The title of lawyer is granted to a duly sworn law licensee, duly registered with a Bar or on the list of the trainees for a Bar. The training course lasts two consecutive years, and at the end of the training a professional training certificate is issued, which makes it possible for its holder to request his enrollment in the rolls of practicing lawyers.

[17] The expression "proxy" designates those individuals who, using certificates manufactured by corrupt notaries, and aided by agents of the police force and of the judiciary, invade the private lives of decent people.

Magistrates

Magistrates are government civil servants tasked with applying the law in court. Magistrates exist at the Supreme Court level, in the Court of Appeals (the Circuit Courts), in the Courts of First Appeals and in the Courts of Peace (the district court). These individuals receive the most blame for the poor performance of the Haitian judicial system.

District Court Magistrates

There are no professional standards in place for Justices of the Peace in local, district courts in Haiti. These judges are not required to work regular hours or to keep regular schedules, and casually leave the bench to attend a meeting about an affidavit. As a result, most Justices of the Peace pad their monthly salaries, since the meager pay that they receive is barely enough to pay the rent.

Many district court magistrates are recruited on a political basis and are in the same situation as members of the Public Prosecutor's office, who are often recipients themselves of political favors from the well connected. These judicial professionals are not recruited on the basis of their overall competence, experience, discipline, integrity, or respect for moral values. They dispense secret justice in line with the conditions of their recruitment.

Dysfunction in the Prosecutor's Office and Courts of Minor Offense (Police Courts)

Ignoring their peace-keeping duties, government prosecutors and their police deputies spend much of their time handling civil issues such as land and rent disputes, private debts and the like. Without any legal justification they issue orders to individuals to appear before a judge with the sole aim of later converting the orders into arrest warrants. This veritable "waltz" of illegal orders inevitably leads to corruption in reaction to the arrests.

The Prosecutor's Office is incapable of playing the primary role assigned to it by law, namely, the prosecution of crimes and misdemeanors. Prosecutors and Deputies in penal matters employ a pernicious technique to shirk their responsibilities. When suspects are brought before the Prosecutor's Office for whatever offense, prosecutors hastily produce indictments and turn suspects over to the Investigative Office (the *Cabinet d'Instruction*). The proper procedure should be the issuance of a direct summons to appear in front of a judge in court. Understandably, this practice fills the Investigative Office with so many cases that the task of the Investigative Judge is made even more difficult.

District Courts (Courts of Peace), in their capacity as simple police courts, possess a similar tendency when handling cases. Justices of the Peace strive for the most part to engage in a process of reconciliation instead of judging simple offenses according to code of criminal procedure regulations. As auxiliaries to the Government Prosecutor, Justices of the Peace can only operate within strict jurisdictional bounds. They should thus be able to judge infractions carefully, retaining only minor infractions and submitting all those infractions that qualify as serious offenses or crimes to the Government Prosecutor. Additionally, certain Justices of the Peace choose to ignore the facts as soon as a financial agreement can be arranged.

These illegal practices lead to real dysfunction across the entire penal system. Justice is generally ridiculed. The accused have no confidence in magistrates who are labeled, even if sometimes unjustifiably, as salesmen of justice.

Although somewhat different, the situation is no better at the level of the Courts and the Tribunals. Cases in the Courts of First Appeal ("*Première Instance*") for example, are completely backlogged, and magistrates make rulings based on personal opinions, in contempt of the Rule of Law.

Criminal Judges

When detainees arrive under arrest at the Prosecutor's Office and are handed over to criminal judges, the court's sluggish operation is in and of itself a deplorable injustice. A study carried out in Haiti's various courts established that the judiciary's performance is unsatisfactory.

More specifically, judicial inefficiency is considerably worsened by an outrageous procedural formalism embodied in the code of criminal procedure. Most of the time the Public Ministry takes all the pains in the world to thwart challenges from the defense lawyers in what are largely frivolous matters. Frequently, the prosecution's failure to present even minimal evidentiary proof obliges judges to release defendants, even when their guilt is abundantly clear to everyone present. Even worse, out of fear of criticism, magistrates simply close their eyes and issue guilty verdicts. Both cases make of a mockery of law and justice.

On the national level, in Courts of Peace as on other jurisdictional levels, judicial inefficiency is characterized by two principal elements:

- A careless and lax approach that confuses the accused and their public defenders.
- Informal deal making in place of legal trial procedures, which produces corruption.

The amount of time judges spend in post-trial deliberations is additional evidence of laxity in the courts. Article 77 of the decree of August 22, 1995 states that "decisions by Justices of the Peace must be returned no more than eight days after civil and commercial cases, and no more than three days after petty crime offenses." This provision remains a dead letter. Justices of the Peace often deliberate for several months before returning decisions.

The situation is no better in higher courts. Months and months can go by before judges render decisions. All too often, cases must be retried due to changes in the legal status of one or both parties.

Article 75 of the decree of August 22, 1995 specifies that judges cannot go on vacation at the end of the judicial year if they have not issued decisions in all matters they handled. The text also states that judges who "fail to do so" are presumed to have resigned. How many judges conform to this provision? Has any magistrate who has violated this provision ever been sanctioned?

The Investigative Office

The Investigative Office should be regarded as the cornerstone of the Haitian penal system. However, because of the practices of the Government Prosecutors' Offices, the Investigative Offices are overloaded with matters that should have been handled by the Criminal Court through direct summons. Moreover, Investigating Magistrates are almost completely incapable of carrying out serious investigations. They have no means of communication, no support staff, and lack even the most elementary materials such as typewriters and photocopiers.[18]

In the Investigative Office, investigations in a majority of the cases are defective and do not lead to any resolution. As a consequence, the courts and the tribunals are swamped with cases they cannot handle. Justice is paralyzed, handicapped by problems of all kinds.

SLOW JUSTICE AT EVERY LEVEL

The Penal Level

Investigative deadlines and the issuance of verdicts in criminal matters are excessively prolonged.[19] This phenomenon causes the

---

[18] The judicial apparatus cruelly lacks the essential equipment for the smooth functioning of justice. From an institutional point of view, the Haitian justice faces many problems, the most crucial of which are: a qualitative and quantitative deficiency in human resources, a lack of financial resources, the state of disrepair of the buildings where the majority of the courts and tribunals of the Republic are located, and a lack of equipment and effective means to carry out investigations.

These problems present innumerable obstacles to the judicial system's functioning, and must urgently be taken into account within the framework of any serious proposals for judicial reform.

[19] Article 9-3 of the International Agreement on Civil and Political Rights states that detention pending trial should be the exception, not the rule. However, in Haiti, long delays in gathering evidence contribute to the lengthening of the duration of detention. The three-month deadline imposed by the Criminal Instruction Code (CIC) to handle the matter is routinely violated. Individuals placed in detention may remain there a year or more before being brought to trial. The State is responsible for ensuring that trials take place without excessive delays. For this to be possible, the State should consider increasing the number of judges that rule on detentions and of equipping them with the

country's detention centers to become clogged, in particular, the National Penitentiary in Port-au-Prince and other prisons in big cities: Cap-Haïtien, Gonaïves, Cayes, Jacmel, Jérémie, Port-de-Paix, Hinche, Saint-Marc.[20]

Political Interference

One of the largest obstacles encountered in the functioning of justice in Haiti remains political interference with the judiciary.[21]

---

means to achieve their mission (material and financial resources, guarantees of investigation powers, etc).

[20] As of February 7, 2007, five thousand thirty (5030) individuals are incarcerated in Haiti. Only seven hundred ninety-two (792) of them have been convicted of a crime, that is to say, approximately 15%. On April 27 2007, the number surpassed to five thousand six hundred forty-seven (5647), an increase of 10.92%, or approximately 617 prisoners in less than three months.

"We have had an increase of more than 200 prisoners per month. If the trend continues, from here until December 2007, the Haitian prison population will likely exceed seven thousand people," predicted Police chief Prévillon Célestin.

Before February 29, 2004, the Haitian State had 21 functional penal institutions throughout the country. Following the events of 2004, three of them - those of Gonaïves, Small-Goâve and Aquin - were destroyed or ransacked by rebels. Fort National, a prison for women and minors, was unused during this time. Currently, the State has approximately 86 cm^2 for each prisoner, whereas, according to international standards, each prisoner should have at his disposal 4 m^2 of living space.

[21] In Haiti, there are numerous examples of political interference with judicial authority or of obstacles placed in the progress of investigations by the executive branch. Commenting in a letter on the investigation of the case of Jean Dominique, killed in the courtyard of his radio station, Radio Haiti Inter, on April 3, 2000, Reporters Without Borders illustrated in its characteristic style some of the political obstacles encountered by the judiciary. Indeed, in this letter addressed January 24, 2002 to President Jean-Bertrand Aristide, Reporters Without Borders (RWB) protested against the non-renewal of Judge Claudy Gassant's mandate in charge of the investigation of Jean Dominique's murder. "The assassination of Jean Dominique and the multiple obstacles placed in the way of the investigation's progress are a symbol of the impunity that reigns in Haiti," denounced Robert Ménard, general secretary of RWB. According to information collected by RWB, Claudy Gassant, whose mandate ended on January 4, 2002, was replaced in a January 23, 2002 presidential decree by magistrates Josua Agnant, Bernard Sainvil and Joachim Saint-Clearly.

The investigation's progress was permanently thwarted. Moreover, several witnesses to the assassination of Jean Dominique died in suspicious

Due to function of the hierarchy in the Government Prosecutor's office, the Minister of Justice has the authority to issue orders and thus has direct influence over the way cases are normally handled.

The Scierie Case: The most recent example was the Ministry of Justice's direct intervention in the case of *La Scierie*, a locality in the city of Saint-Marc where several people died in a political conflict between two armed groups: RAMICOSM and Bale Wouze.[22]

This action led to the release of former deputy Amanus Mayette, who benefited from a *habeas corpus* ruling by the Head of the County Court of Saint-Marc, Attorney Ramon Guillaume. Attorney Hugues Saint-Pierre, the President of the Court of Appeals of Gonaïves, who had been invited to participate in the case, died in a tragic accident three days before the decision.[23]

Justice Minister Gousse: Minister Bernard Gousse's letter to the Head of the Civil Court of Port-au-Prince, Jean-Joseph Lebrun, was another example of political power impeding the judicial process. On December 30, 2004, the Minister Of Justice, Bernard

---

circumstances, which put the police and Haitian authorities directly under suspicion. The investigative magistrate also had to carry out his survey under permanent pressure from police intimidation. The latest incident in a long list occurred December 21, 2001 when a security vehicle from the presidential palace deliberately crashed into the judge's car. Police officers then got out of the vehicle and assaulted the magistrate. In a report published on April 2 2001, RWB denounced the fact that the investigation was all but suppressed on several occasions. In June 2000, Jean Wilner Lalanne, suspected of having served as an intermediary between those who ordered the assassination and the executioners, died in doubtful circumstances after his arrest. In January 2001, the judge ran up against Senate opposition when he asked to call Senator Dany Toussaint as a witness…"

[22] The group, Gathering of the Important Activists of Saint-Mark (RAMICOSM), based in La Scierie, directed opposition against the Neptune/Aristide administration in 2004, while the group Bale Wouze supported Lavalas policy in Bas-Artibonite.

[23] Atty. Hugues Saint-Pierre, President of the Court of Appeal of Gonaïves and Dean of the Faculty of Law in that city, was hit by a van on his way to meet authorities from the Ministry of Justice. Minister of Justice Raymond Magloire, invited to oversee the case by the Senate Commission on Safety and Justice, did not deny the fact of having invited the magistrate but stated he was not aware of it. He said a member of his cabinet had taken the initiative for the meeting.

Gousse, wrote a letter officially ordering investigative magistrates Jean Sénat Fleury and Brédy Fabien to turn over all cases the magistrates were in the process of handling.[24]

In effect, the justice minister did not want to permit the investigative magistrates to issue release orders in the cases of several prisoners accused of crimes against the interior and external safety of the State by the Boniface/Latortue government.[25] As a rationale for his interference, in an interview broadcast on Radio Metropole on Monday, January 10, 2005, the Minister went so far as to claim that the families of the jailed defendants had complained about the slowness of the handling of the cases by the judges who were removed from the case.

Two years before, the group *Friends of Lawyers*, directed by René Julien, sounded a cry of alarm over the state of the judicial system in Haiti. The organization affirmed loudly and clearly that the law is in danger in Haiti, and called on civil servants in the judiciary, law students and human rights defense organizations to observe a one-day strike on Tuesday, May 7, 2002. "*Friends of Lawyers* intends to continue to demonstrate its refusal to operate under the empire of a desecrated judiciary. The Association calls for the establishment of the Rule of Law in Haiti to stop ... this descent into Hell."

The Prosper Avril Affair: The *Friends of Lawyers* initiative came at a moment when a growing number of individuals in the judicial and human rights fields had begun to decry the influence

---

[24] Content of the letter of the Minister for Justice Atty. Bernard H. Gousse to the Head of the County Court of Port-au-Prince Jean Joseph Lebrun: "The Minister for Justice and Public Safety presents to you its compliments and informs you that, taking into account the complaints formulated by many of the relatives of the defendants, relative to the slowness noted in the treatment of the cases submitted to the investigative offices of Judges Jean Sénat Fleury and Brédy Fabien, it is important to hand over these files to other judges in order to normalize the operation of this judicial body. Also, without further delay the Minister would like you to take all these files from the hands of said judges and to submit them to other magistrates."

N.B. Under the Haitian Constitution, only the Superior Council of Magistrates is entitled to engage in disciplinary actions against a judge.

[25] Reference to the case of Gerard Jean Juste.

of the executive branch over the judiciary. These individuals denounced the intimidation of investigative magistrate Henry Kesner Noël in the matter of the *Prosper Avril Affair*, also known as the Piâtre Massacre.[26]

In an interview on Radio Metropole on Thursday, May 2, 2002, one of the members of Mr. Avril's defense team, Attorney Rigaud Duplan, cast doubt on Secretary of State for Public Safety Jean Gerard Dubreuil's assertion that investigative magistrate Henry Kesner Noël had not been pressured to place Prosper Avril's name into the file of the March 12, 1990 Piâtre massacre. In a May 2002 letter to then-Minister Of Justice Jean-Baptiste Brown, Attorney Rigaud Duplan, referring to the Judge Noël's revelations, indicated that Mr. Avril was a prisoner of the Lavalas government and demanded his immediate release. In the letter, Attorney Duplan emphasized "that absent his client's discharge without delay, the case will be sent to the Human Rights Commission of the Organization American States (OAS), this Friday May 3 for whatever purpose it may serve."

Termination of Five Judges: The most striking example of political interference with the Haitian judiciary was the Boniface/Latortue administration's decision to terminate five Supreme Court judges.[27] The decision to fire five Supreme Court justices provoked a thorny conflict between the executive and the judicial branches. Magistrates, lawmakers, members of civil society, and the Council of the Wise (*Le Conseil Des Sages*) ... all mobilized to demand withdrawal of the two unconstitutional presidential decrees that ended the terms of the five Supreme

---

[26] The examining magistrate charged with investigating the case of the Piâtre Massacre that occurred on March 12, 1990, Henry Kesner Noël, denounced the pressures exerted on him by the Secretary of State for Public Safety, Jean Gerard Dubreuil, to introduce Prosper Avril's name into the file of the massacre. Forced to leave the country for safety reasons, Magistrate Noël took refuge in the United States of America where he has been living with his family for more than five years.

[27] In a December 9, 2005 decree, President Boniface Alexandre decided to retire Judges Raoul Lyncée, Luc S. Fougère, Louis Alix Germain, Michel D. Donatien and Djacaman Charles for physical and mental incapacity.

Court judges, who were replaced by five new judges sworn in at the National Palace.[28]

The government's actions were contrary to the prescriptions of articles 174, 175 and 177 of the March 29, 1987 Haitian Constitution.

Article 174: Supreme Court and Courts of Appeal judges are appointed for ten (10) year terms. County Court [judges] are appointed for seven (7) year terms. Their terms begin to run after taking their oaths.

Article 175: Supreme Court Judges are nominated by the President of the Republic from a list of three (3) people per seat submitted by the Senate. Courts of Appeal and County Court judges are appointed from a list submitted by the relevant departmental assembly; Justices of the Peace are nominated from a list prepared by the communal assemblies.

Article 177: Supreme Court, Courts of Appeal and County court judges cannot be removed from office. They can be dismissed only after a legally determined breach of duty or suspended following an indictment. They cannot be assigned to a new post without their assent, even in the event of a promotion. During their term, their service can only be terminated in the event of duly noted permanent physical or mental incapacity.

The issue regarding termination of the Supreme Court Judges can be summarized as follows: Can the Executive Branch, under provisional president Attorney Alexandre Boniface, terminate five Supreme Court Judges and, without a sitting parliament, name five new Judges to fill vacancies at the highest judicial authority in the land? What then about articles 175 and 177? Under article 177, permanently appointed Judges cannot be assigned new posts without their assent, even in the event of promotion. Their service

---

[28] Judges Georges Brace, Henry Michel Auguste, Jules Cantave, Jean Metsguerre Theodore and Bien-Aimé Jean gave their oath in the yellow living room of the National Palace on the evening of Wednesday December 15, 2005. At the end of a short procedure initiated by the Public Minister of the Court Atty. Emmanuel Dutreuil, and the reading of the nomination decree by clerk Balk Andre, the president of the session Atty. Charles Danastor invited the appointed judges to give their oath.

cannot be terminated during their term in office except in the event of duly noted permanent, physical or mental incapacity. These articles state that a judge's career ought to be free from any attempt by the Executive Branch to suspend, to reassign, to terminate or to unilaterally remove a judge. On this basis, article 20 of the decree of August 22, 1995 ordering judges to retire after age 60 is also contrary to the provisions of controlling law.

Article 20 constitutes a serious attack on the principle of judicial independence. According to the terms of article 60 of the Constitution, "each power is independent of the other two with regard to the prerogatives that each exercises separately." In the same way, the Constitution establishes three independent powers without endowing any of them a special right to control or to protect the other.

Rather than moving the country toward democracy, the Executive power's decision to terminate five Supreme Court justices in order to prevent them from working on the SIMEUS /CEP case paved the way to arbitrariness. In choosing to open the doors of the National Palace for the swearing-in ceremony of the five newly appointed judges, the Boniface/Latortue government blatantly violated the principle of the separation of powers that it had sworn to uphold, and committed what was at the time the largest insult ever inflicted on the country's most prestigious institution - the Supreme Court.[29]

---

[29] The Court of Appeals is the Highest Jurisdiction. It has the last word on the law. It arbitrates conflicts over jurisdictions. It judges the facts and the law in every decision rendered by Military tribunals.

The Court of Appeals does not get involved with all the facts of cases. Nevertheless, in all matters other than those submitted to a jury on a second appeal, even in the case of an exception in a matter arising between the same parties, the Court of Appeals that takes the appeal will simply not render a decision and will rule on the basics, with the sections joined. In litigations remanded to it on appeal, The Court of Appeals rules joint session on the constitutionality of laws (Art. 183 of the Constitution).

In the event of dissent between the Legislative power and the Executive power, the Court of Appeals rules in joint session, with all matters suspended. If however the Arbitration Commission does not manage to arrive at a solution, the Court's decision will be final and will be imposed on all parties.

From these examples, one can conclude that the Haitian judicial system functions very poorly; absolutely no transparency exists in its operation. Currently, the manner in which judges are selected and appointed makes the goal of judicial independence impossible to achieve.[30]

Under the supervision of the Minister of Justice, the judiciary holds power in name only. Each new administration presumes *de facto* control over the judicial apparatus and operates in its own interest, completely apart from the principles established by the Constitution and governing law.

The Ministry of Justice

Lack of oversight over the activities of the district courts and county courts is one of the oldest defects in the Haitian judicial system. Because of this lack of oversight, magistrates frequently act in contempt of legislative measures and regulations. They are accountable to no one. This state of affairs has led to deviant behavior by many in the legal community, discrediting the judiciary.

No authority exists within the Ministry of Justice to oversee the proper performance of the Courts and Tribunals, or to ensure truly

---

The Court of Appeals is divided into two sections that sit in separate sessions. They also meet as a General Assembly or as the Superior Council of Magistrates, in cases envisaged by the law. Actually, this last role has not yet been defined. In its ordinary competence, the Court of Appeals accepts in particular appeals drawn from lower-court decisions, appeals court orders and judgments rendered in any matter, and as a last resort from any county court in granting appeals of district court sentences.

The President of the Court of Appeals is the President of the Arbitration Commission. The President of the Court of Appeals is second in line of succession for the State, and replaces the President of the Republic in the event of absence. (Article 149 of the Constitution).

[30] In Geneva, Louise Arbour, High Commissioner of the United Nations for Human Rights (UNHCR), expressed concern over the dismissal of five Court of Appeals judges, saying in her opinion "that in the absence of contrary evidence not produced to date, Haitian authorities seem to have truly attacked the independence of the judicial power." See articles 175, 176 and 177 of the Constitution of March 29, 1987 on the judicial power and the principle of judicial independence.

effective supervision over legal investigations. The Ministry of Justice is satisfied with appointing young people fresh out of university as investigators. In reality these young people, although very enthusiastic, have little chance of success because in addition to their lack of hands-on training and experience, they are not likely to be taken seriously by judicial authorities. Why, then, does the Ministry not consider appointing former judges, former police chiefs and clerks as investigators?[31]

The Ministry also continues to violate certain administrative rules by arbitrarily removing magistrates based on secondhand information. Honest magistrates are frequently removed simply for choosing to respect the law rather than do the Ministry's bidding.[32]

---

[31] It should be recognized that simply by reinforcing the judicial investigation services attached to the Ministry for Justice and Public Safety would do nothing but reinforce the reports of the judiciary's dependence on the executive. That does not mean, however, that a system governing the discipline of magistrates is not necessary. On the contrary, if it is necessary to envisage an equitable procedure for the application of disciplinary actions, it should be in the context of guaranteeing the non-interference of the executive branch.

It is necessary to establish a Superior Council of Magistrates in order to ensure a clear separation between the judiciary and the executive powers, and by assigning it, within the framework envisaged by the Constitution, the functions of selection, formation and discipline of currently sitting magistrates and those in the prosecutor's office.

It would be desirable for the Council to include representation from all levels of the judiciary while remaining open to civil society that could also form a part of it, as certain experiences have demonstrated.

[32] A reference to the decision of June 25, 2001 of the Minister of Justice, Gary Lissade, dismissing investigating magistrate Jean Sénat Fleury in the Belvil case.

"On June 1, 2001, accompanied by the Acting Police chief of the Elco Saint Armand government, the Police superintendent of Port-au-Prince, Samson Auguste, and by ten police officers, I went in the capacity of Investigating Magistrate to Belvil to search a house belonging to Jacques Beaudouin Kétant where 41 kilograms of cocaine and an important amount of money had been found during a previous raid on the residence. One Wista Louis, sought by the police for drug trafficking, lived in the aforementioned house after the seals had been broken.

This operation gave rise to a real scandal in Haitian judicial circles. The Minister of Justice, Gary Lissade considered the search to be illegal. A few days

Judges are asked in good conscience to remain objective, when the Ministry of Justice keeps them enslaved in fact. What kind of independence can one thus expect?

JUSTICE AND CORRUPTION

Corruption is obviously a phenomenon as old as the world, but had not been a dominant concern of the Haitian State until very recently. Nearly a decade ago, the phenomenon became an important topic in political, socio-economic and judicial debates both on the national level and international level, and was the subject of intense media scrutiny. But even though corruption is not a new phenomenon, the nature, degree and extent of measures aimed at controlling it and bringing it to an end have yet to be found.

Corruption does not have a single definition. The most current is that of the World Bank (WB), which says that corruption is "the abuse of a public office in order to obtain a private advantage."

---

later, in a press conference the Minister announced that Investigating magistrate, Jean Sénat Fleury, Acting Police Chief Elco Saint Armand and companions had gone among "people living peacefully in Belvil" to steal jewels, paintings, and shoes and demanded a bribe of 1.5 million dollars. The minister, in contempt of the constitutional requirements (of articles 175 and 177) sent me a letter of suspension." See the report of the School of Law of the University of Miami written by Brian Concannon Jr., Director of the Institute for Justice and Democracy in Haiti (IJDH). The report said: "At the beginning of June 2001, Judge Fleury as caught in the crossfire "between principle and practice," at the time of a search of the house of an alleged drug trafficker, a client of the Minister of Justice of the time, Louis Gary Lissade. The search was legal but angered the Minister. The judge was thus accused of theft and was suspended illegally. A few months later - too slowly but surely - the democratic system corrected itself. Minister Lissade was dismissed and Judge Fleury was restored to his post."

N.B. On June 17, 2003, the Drug Enforcement Administration (DEA) carried out the arrest of Jacques Kétant, extradited from Haiti at the request of the American department in charge of the fight against drugs. He was sentenced to 27 years in prison by a federal court in Miami (Florida). He has admitted to having introduced more than 30 tons of cocaine into the United States over a 12-year period. His two accomplices, Wista Louis, 47, and her husband, Emmanuel Thibaud, were sentenced, the first to 16 years in prison and the second to 12 years and 6 months for drug trafficking in Miami.

The definition supplied more recently by the Council of Europe (EC) broadens it a bit to include the private sector and civil society: corruption includes secret grants of authority and schemes of one kind or another which implicate people in public or private office, who violate duties arising out of their designation as a public servant, a private employee, an independent worker or other relationship, with a view to obtaining illicit advantages of whatever kind for themselves or for others. In a study called *The Fight Against Corruption – An Introductory Guide*, the Canadian Agency of International Development adopted the same definition.

Corruption is indeed the "politics of the belly," to borrow a Cameroonian expression, and it is practiced everywhere in the world. It has been, and continues to be practiced in every place and time. Corruption can take various forms: bribes or under-the-table payments, gifts, swindles, misappropriations, trading of favors, fraud, nepotism, illicit enrichment, embezzlement or drug trafficking. Whether major or minor, whether active or passive, whether merely political, or a small deal negotiated at the corner market, or a "shady deal" contracted on the basis of a promise of a commission or huge fortune diverted from a company, contrary to morality, corruption devastates countries and ravages everyone, in particular the poor.

According to the legal definition, corruption constitutes any unlawful behavior by which an individual solicits, agrees to, or makes an offer to carry out, or to refrain from carrying out, any act in return for favors, benefits, promises, gifts or presents.

The fight against corruption has become a major crusade among international institutions. Over the last several years, organizations like the International Monetary Fund (the IMF), the World Bank (WB), the Organization of American States (OAS), the Inter-American Development Bank (BID), the Organization of Cooperation and of Economic Development (OECD), the United Nations (UN), and Transparency International (TI), have intensified efforts in this fight because they are convinced that the consequences of corruption are disastrous for developing countries.

As a global concern, the twenty-five (25) countries that are signatories to the Inter-American Convention Against Corruption of the Organization of American States (OAS) have targeted corruption. It took effect on March 6, 1997, thirty (30) days from the date the second instrument of ratification was submitted. The Convention was the first multilateral convention on corruption ever negotiated. Within the framework of the fight against corruption, the Convention aims at strengthening co-operation among countries in the Americas.

Adopted two years ago, and ratified by 38 of the 140 signatory countries, including two (2) countries of the European Union, the United Nations Convention Against Corruption, called the Mérida Convention, took effect Wednesday December 14, 2005. According to Transparency International, the primary international nongovernmental organization devoted to the fight against corruption, the United Nations convention is a very important step in the international effort to fight this scourge. For the second time, a multilateral instrument authoritatively established the principle of restitution for unlawfully acquired assets and proposed the introduction of an effective system of mutual judicial assistance.[33]

The Phenomenon of Corruption in Haiti

Corruption is a phenomenon found today in all areas of civic life in Haïti.[34] Nonetheless, the phenomenon is most visible and has the most severe consequences in the judicial system. [35]

The topic of justice and corruption is very controversial and reaches beyond the justice system to society as a whole. The problems involved in judicial corruption are numerous and can be found on multiple levels and among many groups.

---

[33]

http://www.fsa.ulaval.ca/personne/vernag/eh/f/ethique/lectures/sommetcorruptio n.htm

[34] According to a 2004 Transparency International report on the index of reported corruption (IPC), Haiti is one of the most corrupt countries on the planet (155th out of 159).

[35] The Rule of Law expands in an environment of peace, equity, and justice. Unfortunately, our judicial system is very, very sick, corroded by impunity and corruption. Often, we observe that the system does not render justice to whom justice is due. (Jean-Bertrand Aristide, Shalom 2004, Printing works Henry Deschamps, p.170).

Corruption Among Magistrates

Magistrates are human beings with human weaknesses. When placed in a political, social, cultural and economic environment in a country undergoing an identity crisis, where everything is based on material wealth, magistrates are more inclined to lessen their burdens by entering the vicious circle of corruption.[36]

According to the Haitian mindset, it is customary to leave a gift as a sign of respect when in the presence of an authority figure. Some lawyers adopt the same strategy in the Haitian judicial system: "give an envelope to the judge to gain his favor in a judgment."

Corruption stems not only from economic factors, but results from an absence of moral integrity. Moral decline is at the origin of corruption. Admittedly, Haitian judges receive modest incomes. But this weakness alone does not explain the extent of the phenomenon of corruption currently infecting Haitian justice and compromising its essential values.

Rooting Out Corruption

The plague of corruption touches all areas of human activity. At the judicial level, the effects of corruption takes on exponential

---

[36] For Haiti, a preliminary stage in decreasing the extent of corruption in the operation of justice will be to deal with those lawyers and judges who insist on maintaining corrupt and informal methods of practice and application of laws from which they profit. Strict regulations and penalties, as well as professional qualification criteria must be applied to this group of important agents. The development and enforcement of suitable laws in all fields: commercial, civil, criminal, immigration, etc. will constitute part of the first step and beyond. If there exists a field or a group of professionals that will need courage, integrity, qualification and competence, a sense of civic duty and humility for development and implementation of judicial standards, it is indeed in the justice sector in Haiti. The people interviewed within the framework of our study have declared, "Haitians seek a genuine justice system." To honor their wishes and to make rapid advances in developing functional requirements, institutions that can integrate the judicial system in an effective and transparent manner must be treated seriously. It is a field that development agencies and their leaders must enthusiastically support and help to develop, and which citizens must encourage by changing their own behavior. (Tatiana K. Wah, In search of a consensus after 200 years of independence: The structure of the Haitian social system and the challenges of development, printed by New Era Publishing, p. 261).

proportions and constitute a serious threat to the establishment of a democratic State founded on respect for basic human rights.[37] A firm hand is necessary to stop those who corrupt and those corrupted by them. Laws against corruption must be re-examined and modified to meet modern demands.[38]

A new outlook is required in order to make people understand that those who corrupt render no service to magistrates or to the

---

[37] The evil of corruption undermining the country's foundations has shaken Haiti alarmingly. So alarming that national institutions, namely, the Superior Court of Accounts and Administrative Disputes (CSC/CA), the Central Processing Unit for Financial Information (UCREF), the Commission of Administrative Inquiry (ECA), The General Investigation Unit of Finances (IGF), the Unit for the Fight Against Corruption (ULCC) and the National Commission of Public Markets (CNMP) have all assigned themselves the goal of fighting corruption in Haitian public administration, according to their respective missions, each in its own manner.

[38] The battle against corruption was one of the key topics in the speech of May 18, 2007 given by the President of the Republic, Rene Garcia Préval, at a flag ceremony. From the rostrum of the UN at the time of the 62nd National Assembly held in New York, president Rene Préval, in his September 26, 2007 speech, repeated, almost with the same themes, the determination of the current government to fight the plague of corruption: " We are building the means, in Haiti, to face corruption, and we began work to consolidate the structures of the State, and to consider the necessary legal and regulatory reforms so that this endemic evil might disappear from our institutional practices, in politics as well as from commerce."

Also, the President declared that universities, sociologists, leaders, lawyers, political economists, and members of Parliament, in particular, must consider the question. In parliament, legislation relative to corruption must be re-examined and adapted to modern demands.

country.[39] Corrupt justice benefits no one, but paves the way for increased conflict and acts of vengeance.[40]

The fight against corruption requires a host of measures that must be enacted simultaneously.[41] In this light, the following strategies should be adopted:

---

[39] On the economic level, the plague of corruption represents a barrier against the country's development and stability. All in all, it touches funds that were to be used for teaching, investment, and public infrastructure, and often diverts them for private ends. In other words, it prevents developing countries, like Haiti, from attracting foreign investment and creates distortions in the distribution of the capital. Moreover, it is prejudicial against civil society, in particular against the most vulnerable, the poor. Setting itself up as a system, it discourages direct foreign investment and creates a lamentable political instability that has serious effects on the credibility of the State in the eyes of the international community.

[40] In the judicial field, corruption threatens the independence of the judicial power in its impartiality and its equality, and saps democracy and the Rule of Law, which are the principal preconditions for economic growth and the reduction of poverty. The latter impedes fair trials, encourages impunity, and undermines the legitimacy of public authorities, i.e. good governance. At the root of a bad justice system, it creates conflict and the desire for revenge in civil society.

[41] Relevant to the public domain, corruption is contrary to criminal law; it is envisaged and punished in articles 137, 138, 139, 140, 141, 142, 143, and 144 of the Haitian Penal Code. Article 137 punishes corruption in these terms: "Any public servant in the administrative, judicial or military branch, any agent or employee of any public administration who arranges, offers or promises to do something pertaining to his function or employment, including, but not limited to things related to his salary, will be punished with civil sanctions and condemned to a fine of double the value of the approved promise or things received, except that the aforementioned fine cannot be lower than fifty piastres."

On December 19, 2000, Haiti ratified the Inter-American Convention against Corruption, published in the July 18, 2002 # 57 bulletin. Since that date, this convention is an integral part of our legislation. In a decree dated September 8, 2004, the transition government of Boniface Alexandre created a Unit called "**The Unit for the Fight against Corruption (ULCC)**" "tasked with fighting corruption and its manifestations within the framework of Haitian public administration. Now that all the laws are in place, this simply amounts to setting up the actual structures for applying these measures.

Creation of A National Anti-Corruption Watchdog Group

The idea of creating a national anti-corruption watchdog group stems from increased awareness of the perverse effects of corruption felt by all citizens.[42] With few exceptions, the almost completely nonfunctional Superior Council of Magistrates has never taken up the task of punishing rotten and corrupt magistrates. The Council's behavior can be easily explained by the fact that it is made up entirely of magistrates. No one can serve as both judge and jury.

Aggressive solidarity favors impunity. This truth alone justifies the creation of a watchdog group. To preserve neutrality, the group must be made up of members of civil society whose mission is to gather information regarding the facts of corruption, and if the case so warrants, to refer it to a competent authority for punishment. This structure could exist at the local, regional and national level.[43]

If used wisely, an anti-corruption watchdog group, whose existence has now become a necessity, should be viewed as a compelling mechanism that will allow citizens to free themselves from subordination to the unethical conduct of public figures.[44]

---

[42] Morally, the system of corruption perverts the ethical relationship of reciprocity, constitutes a direct attack on the intangible core of human rights; because of its endemic character brought about by the perverse acceptance of the violation of the principle of equality, it undermines the principle of confidence constitutive of the Rule of Law. (Marco Borghi, law professor at the University of Freibourg, Switzerland).

[43] Civil society is regarded as the pillar of democracy. It plays an effective part in the fight against impunity and the defense of individual freedoms. The only hope of succeeding with social demands lies in the number, in the quantity of, people who can be

mobilized around an idea, a defense. Also, the press, defense associations of the rights of the person, intellectuals, voluntary groupings, various experts on national life, lawyers' groups, the national association of magistrates, etc., constitute lobbies for the development of a structural reinforcement of justice. This civil society must be perceived as formulating proposals or even demands on the State for a major transformation of society. It is thus a very significant agent in the reform process of our apparatus of justice.

[44] See the order of October 13, 1983 fixing the procedures and the methods of naming of the agents of public office, and the law of September 19, 1982 establishing the general statutes of public office.

Introduction of a Transparent Inspection System

A transparent inspection system would consist of designated specialists who publish and comment on judicial decisions.

These specialists would denounce cases of judicial abuse, and public opinion would be sufficiently informed of the practices of members of the judiciary.[45] These specialists could be given a precise mandate granting them access to evidence in cases before various jurisdictions.

Conduct a Massive Media Campaign

The media campaign must be carried out nationwide, and non-governmental organizations (NGOs) should be actively involved in the process. Education, training, awareness and communication are required to eradicate judicial corruption. This difficult work requires everyone to commit to behavioral change.

Respect for the Code of Ethics

In order for professional ethical standards to be scrupulously respected, the judicial body must undergo a process of moral development and consciousness-raising. This process should appeal to the morality and sense of civic duty of those in charge of the distribution of justice, in particular to Magistrates.

Judges hold enormous power, a fact that ought to inspire them to be just. Judges should thereby feel obliged to deliver a robust justice. In rendering decisions, judges should obey only their consciences, according to their innermost convictions. They should not yield to external pressure. Similar to the priesthood, indeed, it is difficult to imagine an analogous profession. The judge's role must be strengthened and carried out in complete

---

[45] So that the people might be trustful of the will or of the ability of the State to sanction abuses, it is important that the authorities make public the results of investigations. Official press statements must announce suspensions, removals, in short, the sanctions taken against civil servants of justice without distinction. This method will make it possible for the public to build a case of abuses that were sanctioned, and as for the authors, to become aware of their acts. Thus, the people will be trustful of the will and of the ability of the State to put a stop to cases of violations committed by agents of the judiciary.

conscientiousness and with full knowledge of its ramifications. Judges' rulings must carry the seal of sincerity, exactitude, and integrity in every case, without the slightest hint of bias.

CHAPTER II:
REFORMING JUSTICE

Often depicted as an open wound, the failure of justice in Haiti is the subject of numerous contemporary commentaries. In order to allow Haitians to live in a just and democratic society, and to allow Haiti to reenter the community of so-called modern nations, now more than ever the need for reform is clear.[46] Is it not justice that builds nations?

---

[46] If there is one word that has been repeated almost incessantly even in higher echelons in connection with justice, it is certainly "failure. " The Haitian and foreign specialists are unanimous in recognizing the dysfunction of the Haitian judiciary apparatus. "The reform of justice and the reform of the police force must go hand in hand", declared Prime Minister Jacques Edouard Alexis at the time of his declaration of General Policy in June 2006.

"... The objective in the field of Safety and Justice is clear. We should take back our full sovereignty. To reach this result, we must make peace among ourselves. The Government will devote to it all desired efforts for finally mastering this culture of peace which is at the same time the source and the guarantor of the rights and duties of the citizen, and which is at the heart of the new system of values and behaviors that require our determination for a new departure towards a durable and constant democracy. However, it will not be able to happen by itself; it will call upon all the components of society and will persevere in the practice of dialogue and the collaboration that characterized our approach since the elections of last February 7. Thus, the participation of the people will contribute to the introduction of this culture of peace.

It will be necessary for us for some time to come to use the support of friendly countries to guarantee the stability of the State and the safety of the people. This support will have to allow us to professionalize the national police force of Haiti, to reach a level of sufficient qualified manpower and to equip it with the means necessary for the performance of its duties.

A police force is effective only if the organization of justice is able to meet its needs adequately. In fact, it is all the problems of the criminal justice system that are concerned. The Government recommends an integrated approach Justice/Police to equip the country with a judicial system that is responsible, professional, and able to give confidence again and to guarantee the safety of the citizens, to fight effectively against smuggling, drug dealers and criminalized gangs. The police force must also ensure control of the borders and

But what does judicial reform really mean? Putting aside purely academic definitions in order to truly appreciate the living reality of the expression, judicial reform is a set of measures adopted in the field of justice, intended to thwart those who do not respect the law, to secure the safety of decent people, and to guarantee universal rights. In this sense, strictly speaking, no judicial reform can ever be accomplished definitively. The right to justice and the rights inherent in justice entail, in truth, a permanent quest in a democratic state that seeks to improve these rights by taking account of the evolution of the social fabric and the demands of modernity.

To speak of reform is undoubtedly to draw attention to the deplorable state of justice in Haiti and to the need for all stakeholders to collaborate in finding solutions. For this reason,

---

immigration, considerable challenges, with a coastline as large as ours and borders so difficult to reach because of rugged terrain.

The Superior council of the National police force of which I am the statutory President will be responsible for the whole of the security and justice program, including the management of the support coming from MINUSTAH." However, here is a question to be asked: will Jacques Edouard Alexis manage to carry out the judiciary reform as promised in his declaration of General Policy? The Prime Minister seems determined, but the system must face the obstacles of corruption, the lack of means, the administrative delay in handling judiciary cases and especially the problems involved in the training of magistrates and the education of the defendants.

It is enough to hear the claims and to read the last three years' assessments - all the confused courts. The facts jump out at the reader: 80% of prisoners are in detention pending trial, the investigations on the level of the Offices of Investigation are dragging on at length, the large majority of the decisions of our Tribunals and Courts are incoherent. In short, the Haitian judiciary apparatus is badly lacking confidence in the eyes of the defendants.

The report, already old, practically has unanimous acceptance today. All the debates turn around the charter of the reform.

Accepting the idea according to which there could not be democracy without justice, the Préval/Alexis Government made the judiciary charter one of its priorities. Indeed, several bills were filed for a vote with the Parliament. The Government decided to carry out a merciless struggle against the plague of drug and corruption. In short, against insecurity.

But, the same question always remains as the order of the day: Has the Government really understood the problems of judiciary reform in Haiti?

arriving at a mutual understanding of the methodology of judicial reform is required, which will reveal the necessary steps to be taken, how to undertake such reform, and will delineate each stakeholder's role.

What must be done? In order to accomplish judicial reform in Haiti, the Head of State must first choose to promote justice as one of the priority issues of his administration, must possess the will to make profound changes in the justice system, must be courageous enough to carry out such reforms, and must seek the means (physical, material, and financial) to radically transform the national justice system by choosing to correct not just past misunderstandings, but to plan a general reform program that stems from a national vision where justice plays a balancing role among the nation's great social, political and economic forces.[47]

The government has two choices in commencing such reform: a minimalist option and a comprehensive option.

A minimalist reform of justice requires a social pact to equitably distribute the nation's riches. In practice, this would mean asking magistrates and judicial servants to accept low wages while ignoring the superior treatment of those public servants who are more politically connected.

The minimalist option is clearly disadvantageous. This type of reform will not identify the best candidates for judgeships, of whom many will be attracted to careers as attorneys, or to the "international field." A young lawyer today earns five to ten times more in the latter field than what he could earn on the bench. The Ministry of Justice must discuss the critical issue of the feasibility of minimalist reforms with international partners.

But there is a second option, which consists of attracting the best judicial minds to the bench. Obviously, a price must be paid to achieve this. The government could immediately eliminate excess staff and empower groups of dedicated, hard-working professionals possessed with a detailed understanding of the organization to take over roles where others have previously done more harm than good.

---

[47] In Haiti, the reform of the judicial system is impossible to circumvent, when the judicial system is not, quite simply, there to be rebuilt.

These individuals would have to be recruited along private sector lines according to individual merit (academic training, experience, work skills). They would represent, for example, students in the judiciary who have been trained specifically to investigate cases, to conduct adequate research and to assemble evidence to submit to a presiding magistrate.

Reform of the Haitian justice system should revolve around the following axes:

INSTITUTIONAL INDEPENDENCE OF JUDGES

After devoting Article 59 to the separation of the three powers, the 1987 Constitution constructs, from article 174 onward, a device that should make it possible for magistrates on the bench to be free from the secular influence of the executive branch. However, in practice, the reality is quite different. Not provided for by any means whatsoever are the material and psychological preconditions of independence. In order to obtain a position in the judiciary one must first go through the Ministry of Justice. The same Ministry controls promotions and removal of magistrates, and controls even their slightest actions. The Ministry's authorities maintain a tight hold on the reigns of the judiciary.[48]

TRAINING AND COMPETENCY

Only properly trained and qualified professionals can accomplish judicial reform, which raises the issue of inculcating a

---

[48] The judicial Power faces operational difficulties. The naming of magistrates and their promotion, judiciary protection of the Justices of the Peace and the officers of the Prosecutor, the dysfunction of the

Superior Council of the Judges and the absence of autonomous budgeting constitute obstacles to the exercise of the Judicial Power and reinforce its dominance by the executive at the organizational level.

The problems of naming and dismissing judges, determination of the vacation and holidays of the Courts and Tribunals, the question of career and the internal rules of the Ministry for Justice, are many of the indications that establish the influence of the Executive on the Judiciary at the institutional level.

program of basic legal and professional training for judicial executives.

The School for Magistrates contemplated in the Constitution to train judges and other judicial administrators has no support from the executive branch.[49] The College has a bad reputation among a group of lawyers who later became Justice Ministers, who believe the college produces corrupt and easily manipulated magistrates.

"In the final analysis, Haitians could have trained magistrates within the framework of a specialization in the Faculty of Law of the State University of Haiti. When the Constitution discusses the creation of a School for Magistrates (art. 176), it does not prohibit integration of such an institution within an already existing structure. On the contrary, it would be easier and less expensive, and that would help us avoid humiliation," said Henri Dorléans, ex-Minister of Justice.

It should be noted immediately that the School for Magistrates is disliked because the executive branch does not possess the will to create a strong, independent judiciary with honest and qualified magistrates. Each successive administration carefully monitors the judicial system so as to not lose control over even one member.

Having described the problem, the question now is: what is required to strengthen the independence of the judiciary?

In their deliberations, judges should not be subject to any pressure from outside sources. They should obey only their own consciences and their inner convictions when applying the law. The political power should never interfere with the judicial power.

---

[49] A School For Judges was created by article 176 of the Constitution of March 29, 1987. The School began in 1995 as a training center, supported largely by international cooperation, for "emergency" training of short duration for the judges and government prosecutors.

Although not enjoying a statutory standing yet, there were three regular promotions of approximately (139) magistrates graduated during the programs of the initial training programs and hundreds of personnel from the judiciary profited from the training courses in the EMA.

Our country's Constitution declares that the judicial power is independent from the other powers.[50]

The concept of irremovability must be strictly respected because judges who are afraid for their positions do not render justice. Agents in charge of the distribution of justice must be protected by statutes and thereby made safe from arbitrary impositions.[51]

Parliament and the Executive power adopted a certain number of laws and decrees that subordinate the Judicial Power to the Executive and Legislative powers (decree of August 22, 1995).

The decree of August 22, 1995 relating to criteria for judicial nominations should be modified to add moral character and fitness requirements.

The same decree should also be modified, and concurrently, the Constitution should be amended to guarantee the principle of judicial irremovability once in office.

---

[50] The Haitian Constitution contains the democratic principles of separation of the powers and the primacy of the rule of the law for all Haitian people, including the principle of judicial independence. However Haitian governments in practice never have respected the letter or the spirit of the Constitution. The judicial system has almost always been subject to the administrative, budgetary whims and personnel of an excessively dominating executive power. (Judiciary Independence in Haiti, June 2002, Bernard Gousse).

[51] See articles 174,175,176 and 177 of the Haitian Constitution of March 29, 1987 defining the judicial power and treating the principle of the irremovability of magistrates. Under article 177, the irremovable judges cannot be the subjects of new assignment without their assent even in the event of promotion. Their service cannot be terminated during their mandate except in the event of permanent physical or mental incapacity duly noted. This results that the career of the Magistrate is exempt from all suspension measures, from being made available, of being replaced, retired or dismissed, decided unilaterally by the Executive power. On this point, article 20 of the decree of August 22, 1995 on the judicial organization foreseeing the possibility of retiring judges who are 60 years old is contrary to the provisions of the basic law. The article in question carries a serious attack on the principle of the independence of the function of the judiciary.

Moreover, revision of the law concerning the Superior Council of Magistrates is recommended to bring the statute in conformity with international standards.[52]

Inter alia, the following texts must be finalized:

• The Law on the status of Magistrates.

• The Law on the Superior Council of Magistrates.

• The Law on the School for Magistrates.

• The Law on Judicial Ethics.

JUDICIAL INDEPENDENCE AND AUTONOMY

A law guaranteeing judicial independence is necessary for the healthy administration of justice.[53] Such independence can be assured only by respecting certain criteria:

---

[52] The law of August 17, 1998 concerning judicial reform puts in the very first row of its objectives the reorganization of the Superior Council of the Judges as the management of the judiciary and guarantor of the independence of the judiciary. This same element is taken up again among "the great choices" of the governmental Action plan of May 1999, such that it is obvious that the judicial power currently is suffering, in formal and informal ways, from the heavy and sometimes authoritative supervision of the executive branch.

Thus, a reform of justice should inevitably come about through the institutionalization of the independence of the judicial power relative to the executive power through the establishment of an administration of a really autonomous judiciary in accordance with the wishes of the Constitution of 1987. Once again, this reform should not ignore the existence of common law. In short, Haitian leaders should think of working out a plan of reform of our judicial system that conforms to our cultural and ancestral historical values.

Therefore, it will be in vain to increase the number of the courts, to multiply the number of judges and to quadruple their wages, without the independence of the judicial power and the harmonization of the two components of the Haitian law. Any such attempt at judiciary reform will be vitiated and incomplete. (See the new law in progress on the Superior Council of the Judiciary).

[53] The non-existence of a really independent judicial power was characterized by the concentration of operations at the level of the Ministry for Justice. The installation of a Superior Council of Judges must make it possible for such a body to be centered on its administrative duties and to intervene in a more rational way in the management of the Courts of Peace and the prosecutors'

a. Improve the salaries of judicial personnel;[54]

b. Develop and approve a Judicial Code of Ethics;

c. Guarantee job security;

d. Require adequate skills, and develop transparent, objective selection and nomination procedures;

e. Ensure objective and transparent judicial career path procedures (for promotions and transfers);

f. Require objective and transparent administrative and judicial procedures;

g. Protect freedom of expression and of association of judges;

h. Guarantee effective and equitable execution of judicial decisions;

i. Provide ongoing and adequate judicial training and education;

j. Improve access to prior jurisprudence and legal scholarship for judges;

Rich and varied research materials, job descriptions and training manuals must be provided to all jurisdictions to compensate for the lack of training and of specialization of magistrates. To meet the needs of the profession, judicial executives must receive advanced training courses. These trainings should lead to judicial specialization because the profession must be empowered to follow the rhythms of environmental, political, social, economic and cultural change. Magistrates should be trained with regard to the concerns of the times.[55] Training will necessarily lead to

---

offices. Also, the adoption of a law guaranteeing the independence of judges is clearly necessary for a healthy administration of justice.

[54] Nowadays, the need for revising the salary schedule of Haitian Magistrates and for allotting them benefits is essential. This design would allow the judge, no longer receiving starvation wages, to abstain from taking offers of bribes that are very current forms of interference in the development process of judgments. Here, to repeat Mrs. Mirlande Manigat: " It is necessary to keep the magistrates safe from their own passions driven by the material needs of life. "

[55] Training for judiciary staff was a priority area of involvement at the beginning of international support in 1995, especially on behalf of the United States and of France, which maintain a marked interest in this field. The United States, in addition to renovation work on the buildings of the School of the Judiciary took

specialization in specific legal areas, which would, without a doubt, result in higher quality rulings.

ADEQUATE PAY FOR MAGISTRATES

Magistrates' living and working conditions must be improved. It goes without saying that a magistrate in financial need is much easier to corrupt, because a hungry person cannot resist temptation. Magistrates, the ones charged with judging their peers, must work in optimal conditions and receive respect from all areas of society.

ACCESS TO JUSTICE FOR ALL

This is one of the great principles of justice in Haiti. Justice is a public service, and magistrates are remunerated by the State. Justice must be perceived as such, as much by those who are

---

charge of a large part of the expenses of operating the School at the beginning and during the following years. They took part in the beginning with the management of the School, the design of the training programs and provided teachers as one important financial contribution for the expenses of the pupils and their allowances for the Haitian trainers.

Training is the priority area of involvement by France in the sector of justice in Haiti. It brought an important support to the School in particular through the supply of computer, teaching and office materials as well as judiciary works, the assignment of a French magistrate and a contribution to the training of the students (per diem of the student magistrates, allowances for the tutors and trainers). With the aim of training trainers, France also took charge of the training of Haitian lawyers in France at the School of the Judges of Bordeaux and the International Institute of Human Rights of Strasbourg as well as clerks with the School of the Clerks Offices of Dijon. It also organized several training courses for Justices of the Peace.

Canada supported some training courses and supported installation of an information center. It provided computer and office materials as well as judiciary works.

The MICIVIH in time also supported the School for Judges by its regular participation in the training courses, in particular as regards human rights; and UNICEF organized several seminars within the framework of the protection of the Rights of the Child.

Unfortunately the Haitian authorities did not understand the need for these programs of improvement for magistrates and the executives of justice. After only three years, the School for Judges closed its doors as a training program.

trained and paid to render it as by those who seek it. For this reason, justice must meet, at least, three requirements: accessibility, hospitality, and satisfaction.

Accessibility

As a public service, justice must be accessible.[56] However, in Haiti two walls separate justice from those it judges: distance and cost. A peasant who lives in Gresseau, a locality in the heights of Montrouis, must travel for at least five hours before reaching the

---

[56] The principal criterion for evaluating a judicial system is to know whom it concerns. In Haiti, formal justice is unaware of in a structural way more than two thirds of the population. Indeed, there does not exist currently any presence of an unspecified judiciary apparatus on the level of basic territorial subdivision that is the commune section. However, it is on this level that the essence of the daily life of the majority of citizens is played out.

Consequently, one cannot speak any longer about a dysfunction but about a central problem of justice in Haiti, namely its absence in fact for a great majority of the people. The contact held with the formal apparatus existing on the level of communal centers could not in any case, not now, nor even if it had suddenly been improved in the future, fill this institutional vacuum which does nothing but worsen the ongoing destruction of traditional society. Besides the same problem arises in the city for the people who have come as a result of rural migration who currently are squeezed into immense zones of informal dwellings without any service of justice, even though the services are definitely closer by. There is only one court of peace for the three hundred and thousand (300.000) inhabitants of Cité Soleil and the territorial limits of its competence are not clearly set.

To make justice accessible to all, two ways are possible to improve the current situation by taking into account the limited means there are at hand: either seek to reach an acceptable level of quality of service rendered to the customers of the defendants (estimated at 25% of the people), or seek to ensure a less sophisticated service but extended to all citizens.

If the existing resources do not make it possible to answer these two objectives at the same time, it is recommended to choose a solution which will make it possible to ensure, at best, the presence of judicial services close to each citizen, whatever his economic level or his culture. This combines the general objectives that the Regional Program of Justice of UNDP set itself for the Latin America and the Caribbean. This choice is due to the need for putting an end little by little to the practices that permanently maintain a hostile duality within Haitian society. If such an objective seems to exceed the dimension of justice alone, it constitutes no less a special means to be attained, in particular, because of the symbolic impact of such measures.

nearest local court. Any framework for judicial reform should consider the possibility of itinerant judges who travel to various communities on market day, or explore the option of neutral community-based mediators who possess legal training.

Regarding cost, justice is practically free, but only as far as the law is concerned. Ask any accused person how much it will cost to obtain a report from the Justice of the Peace, or ask a lawyer how much he charges clients for an act of adoption, or how much an applicant must pay for an action by the court. The answers will quickly convince you that only the rich have access to justice in Haiti.

Hospitality

Justice must be welcoming. Our halls of justice must provide hospitable, welcoming service. A hall of justice should feel palpably different from a market or a factory.[57] Co-operation from Canada deserves recognition for contributing to making people feel welcome via the construction of fourteen Courts of First Appeal buildings across the country. But Justices of the Peace should also be placed in buildings worthy of bearing the name "Tribunal".[58]

The linguistic problem that impedes access to justice for the majority of Haitians must also be solved. In effect, a majority of correctional or criminal cases are pleaded in French, a language

---

[57] Often the public compares the Courts and Tribunals in Haiti with shops in which justice is sold to highest bidder. Thus, the citizen who seeks to obtain the services of justice can believe he is in a market by putting his feet into a Court of Peace. Invaded by a "team of desperadoes": Power brokers, exploitative clerks, foreign agents... he does not have another choice except to quickly leave the place to avoid being strangled.

[58] All the apparatus of formal justice in Haiti depends primarily on both the use of writing and of French, whereas 60% of the population is illiterate and hardly 10% is likely to use French. In spite of the efforts carried out since the introduction of Creole into the Constitution of 1987, the barrier of the means of expression and language contributes to move the majority of people away from the apparatus of justice.

that the majority of the accused do not understand either because they are illiterate or because they have very little education.[59]

Satisfaction

Lastly, as a public service, justice must give satisfaction to the person to be judged or, even better, he must at least feel that the system did its best.

In Haiti, the great principles of justice are not applied judiciously:

---

[59] Nearly three quarters of Haitian people are located today separated from access to official justice. It happens that this excluded part corresponds both to the rural world and to the sector of informal urbanization born out of rural migration. The rural part is almost completely deprived of any security service, the units of police force being stationed exclusively in average and small urban centers.

De facto Rule of Law of these two great masses of people is exercised mainly on the basis of informal law which controls in particular common law marriages, the exercise of the property rights and the revenue from land (rural and urban); these non-codified rules often enter into conflict with the official law based on the Napoleonic code which obeys a basically different logic. Haiti is, in fact, a country with a double judiciary order. This shouldn't pose problems if the Haitian State were recognized as being juridically plural. However, the official system does not recognize the existence of customary or informal law and this latter one is ignored and, with it, most of the people, which governs its social functions according to this parallel set of standards.

Official law having hardly changed for a hundred and fifty years has been little by little, because of the sometimes contradictory complexity of its own laws, practically incapable of solving litigations that create a burden now on its courts and condemn them to paralysis. For lack of judiciary structures close by, people are therefore incapable of solving the essentials of its specific conflicts. In the absence, for the moment, of a rural police force, this conflicting situation is likely to degenerate constantly toward violent solutions.

Normally, the majority of these litigations belong to the nearest Court of Peace (the commune or the district). Nevertheless, the problems of operation with which these are faced - due in particular to a lack of necessary means - the same as their distance, restricts their ability considerably to answer the ever-increasing demands of the people.

The Principle of Access to Rights

The right to be heard by a judge, and the right to have one's case examined by a judge, are the basic elements of access to rights. This principle applies to all individuals regardless of nationality, age, sex or standard of living. It also includes the right of assistance from a translator and to be represented by the defender of one's choice.[60]

The Right to a Fair Trial

All persons have the right to be judged in compliance with the law by an independent and impartial judge. The trial must respect the principles of adversarial debate and the right to an adequate defense.

The Principle of Exemption from Payment

The absence of a public legal assistance system with sufficient resources makes it impossible to guarantee that the accused, particularly those who are economically disadvantaged, will benefit from a lawyer at all stages of the penal process, as provided for in the Constitution of 1987, and according to international standards. With the aim of earning as much money as possible, lawyers are tempted to accept too many cases to the detriment of their clients. Poorly qualified, inadequately remunerated lawyers are detrimental to the interests of justice.

Article 24 of the decree of March 29, 1979 regulating the legal profession provides simply that a lawyer in training "can be selected for service in the defense of defendants and the accused; " but such timely legal aid does have its disadvantages. Some critics think that it weakens the defense of the accused insofar as lawyers

---

[60] Judiciary or judicial aid is an institution which provides poor people resources sufficient to be exempted from paying the expenses and the fees of the judicial administration whose cooperation is necessary to obtain certain advice related to lawsuits or, if necessary, to plead in front of the courts: this help does not exist in Haiti in an institutional and permanent way. Institutionalized judiciary aid is not yet set up to allow the poor obtain State assistance for whole or part of the expenses of a lawsuit.

in training often have little experience, and can only be seen as bargain basement advocacy.

Visit the prisons of Haiti where more than three quarters of prisoners are detained illegally; ask the majority of citizens who don't even dare to bring their cases to court; finally consult those with judgments in their favor but who cannot get satisfaction, and you will get an idea of the frustrations created by the system.[61]

It is not enough to merely adopt new laws: they must be applied. In order to restore the credibility of the judicial apparatus, and to reestablish trust and to give confidence to Haitian citizens who call out, with hue and cry, for the outright destruction of a system that, according to them, is too corrupt and too partisan to deliver justice, justice must be made accessible to all.[62]

Accessibility can be made possible only by:

   a. Education for all those to be judged;
   b. Legal assistance for the most deprived;
   c. Establishment of a swift, straightforward, effective yet flexible justice system for the Haitian people.

---

[61] The fact of throwing your political opponents in a prison in Haiti does not only reduce them to silence, it can just as easily kill them. In January 2005, the 3rd Circuit of the Federal Court of Appeal of the United States declared that there was no doubt that the conditions in the prisons in Haiti "are really miserable and inhuman."

Tuberculosis and other diseases are endemic, the care of health and food insufficient. Certain cells are so packed that the prisoners sleep in turn on the floor. Misery is intentional! In November 2005, the civil servant of the Program of the United Nations for the Development in charge of work in the Haitian prisons resigned over the refusal of the Haitian government to accept international assistance to improve prison conditions.

Murder can also be intentional: "On December 1, 2004, while Colin Powell was visiting the National Palace of Haiti, the police force counteracted an unarmed protest in the prison with blasts from automatic weapons in the cells. The Government says about ten prisoners were killed whereas independent groups of human rights and journalists claim a much higher number. "

[62] It is enough to be convinced by referring to the current distribution of the courts throughout all the territory and the number of judges currently functioning per capita of inhabitants.

In this context, alternative methods of conflict resolution such as reconciliation, mediation, and arbitration should be encouraged and supported in order to reduce the workload of the State judicial system.[63]

---

[63] The promotion of a system of "barebones justice" and its acceptance by the courts and the administration could involve a reduction of the level of the conflicts thanks to simple mechanisms, of proximity, managed by the population itself and, that, at a reduced or quasi non-existent cost. These observations are based on very interesting practices and experiments: At the level of the formal judicial system, and in particular at the level of government commissioners and their substitutes and that of the Justice of the Peace, the law envisages recourse to reconciliation. However, this appears among many of the other prerogatives of this judge caught between multiple responsibilities and who is in addition a judiciary police officer. Those who are in contact with rural environment and know it, all point out the existence of regulating mechanisms of this nature. In practice, it is often a personality recognized by the group for sound moral authority who plays this part, but it is perhaps also the hougan (voodoo), the priest (catholic), Pastor (Protestant) or the "lakou chief."

It is while relying on such mechanisms that, during the years 1997 - 2002 some very encouraging attempts at systematization of practices of alternative resolution of conflicts were carried out by:

a. - Project SOSYETE (financed by USAID), within the framework of its interventions near the basic communities.

b. - MICIVIH, within the context of its support of the actions of Judges of the Peace of Artibonite.

c. - INARA (National institute of Land reform), within the context of land conflicts.

d. - Peace Brigades International (PBI), which carried out education activities on behalf of the MICIVIH and wrote one book of guidelines for reconciliation.

These experiments show that this line of action is promising and makes up a part of the number of initiatives that led to satisfactory results. While being based on these results, it is a question of gradually again taking these pilot experiments through the country with objectives as:

• To promote the resolution of conflicts through negotiation by using reconciliation and mediation as techniques.

• To support the organizations of civil society by helping them to identify the sources of conflicts and to manage them through the techniques of mediation and negotiation.

• To support the institutions of the State that work in the rural and familial sector so, either to set up programs for conflict resolution, or to reinforce the already existing mechanisms.

• To promote with the Justices of the Peace and of the government commissioners, the use of the reconciliation in the current judiciary framework.

• To promote the training of mediators, members of civil society who, in their villages or communities, will be able to provide their services voluntarily.

• To support the adoption of legislative measures and/or directives emanating from the Ministry for Justice and Public safety, relating to the way of using mediation in criminal matters.

• To develop a research on the range and the contents of the Haitian common law and its modes of reconciliation. (read Barthelemy Gerard. Country Outwards, test on the rural universe in Haiti, 2nd ED. Editions Henri Deschamps, Port-au-Prince, 1989).

CHAPTER III:
RECOMMENDATIONS FOR
JUDICIAL REFORM IN HAITI

Two commissions undertook large-scale work on judicial reform; first, the National Commission on Truth and Justice, whose 1995 report contains interesting recommendations for the reform of judicial institutions, and second, the Preparatory Commission For the Reform of the Law and Justice (CPRDJ) (1997-1999) that produced, in addition to several working papers, a Document of General Policy, Strategic Planning and Short-Term Action Plan. The Document of General Policy of the CPRDJ analyzed the context of judicial reform and civil society's requirements with regard to the administration of justice, and proposed a new model of justice and a strategy for intervention.

The recommendations made here are not divergent from those suggested by Haitian lawyers and by foreign analysts, who are unanimous in recognizing the dysfunctional character of the Haitian judicial system and the need for reform.

The recommendations target five main areas:

ESTABLISHING EFFECTIVE JUDICIAL INDEPENDENCE

1. Short-Term Reforms

a. Renovate the buildings that house the courts of the Republic, in particular the local courts.

b. Raise salaries of judicial personnel.[64]

---

[64] The reform of justice in Haiti does not raise only technical problems. It is necessary also to focus on the question of management to raise for the justice executives in particular the question of wages. The starvation wage of judges was always evoked as being one of the causes of corruption in the judiciary apparatus. A Justice of the Peace, especially present in the cities and the villages of the backcountry must find a way to live with less than 200 American dollars per month. The average wages of the Haitian judge are approximately 15.000

c. Introduce courses in ethics and judicial responsibility for the entire judicial staff.

d. Provide courts with the furniture, materials and office supplies essential to properly functioning judicial institutions.[65]

---

thousand gourdes per month, which is approximately $400 American dollars, which is much lower than decent wages and supports corruption directly. The absence of professional and truly independent judges has a catastrophic effect on the system. While supporting corruption, this situation also encourages persons responsible for infringements on human rights who lay out money or other means of influence to think that they can act with impunity. The very weak remuneration of the judges, in addition to the fact that it makes them more vulnerable to corruption, lowers their social status; it is more difficult for them to exercise their functions without fear because it is easy to intimidate them or to influence them.

A correct remuneration must be guaranteed for the judges.

N.B. As a Temporary Justice of the Peace in Montrouis from 1987 to 1991, I was getting from the Haitian State as monthly pay a check in the amount of 864 gourds, less than 40 American dollars at the time.

[65] The strategy of intervention of the international community has consisted since 1995 of devoting the essence of its efforts of support to the urgent operation of the existing judicial system in order to fight impunity and to maintain the order and safety, the questions of institutional reform and the texts being deferred about the means and the long run. The priority needs identified at the very beginning in this field have been primarily material needs (restoration and construction of the courts) and the needs for judiciary staff training (judges of peace, examining magistrates and government commissioners). The Courts and Tribunals received very important support from the international community for the restoration and the construction of buildings, for example, for their operation. Courts of Peace were the object of special attention on behalf of the United States, which drew up a complete inventory and proceeded with many renovation and construction projects. France also financed the restoration of several courts of peace as well as the construction of three of them. By means of a loan from the Inter-American Bank of Development, the Haitian State built 14 courts of peace.

The fourteen county courts and Appeal Courts outside of Port-Au-Prince as well as the juvenile court of Port-au-Prince were entirely renovated or newly built with the support of Canada. Various projects and programs of support for the operation of the courts and appeals courts were set up in particular by the United States and Canada. The support of the United States consisted of logistical assistance with the courts of peace and continuing education programs in jurisdiction for the judges of these courts provided by experienced tutors (23 courts of peace and 2 county courts); the set up of registers of files in 83 courts of peace and 2 land courts; a support for 10 appeals courts by supplying office

Our judicial system severely lacks the essential equipment required for sound management of legal matters. The judicial apparatus should be computerized so that certain decisions are not manipulated.[66] Likewise, all jurisdictions must be equipped with rich, varied and up-to-date research materials and periodicals. Each court must be granted free subscriptions to official legal journals. All of these measures constitute an incentive against corruption, because magistrates will not need to spend their own funds to keep themselves current with the latest jurisprudence.

2. Medium-Term Reforms

a. Revise the decree of August 22, 1995 on judicial organization by harmonizing it with the 1987 Constitution, thereby reinforcing access to the judiciary.

---

equipment and the installation of a system of recording, treatment and follow-up of the files (criminal justice system) as well as a support with the installation of the Office of Control of Preventive detentions (BUCODEP) with the National Penitentiary.

For its part Canada carried out the staff training for 14 county courts that it renovated or built and furnished with the installation with management systems, in particular a system of recording, word processing and follow-up of files (civil branch). France also provided material support to the investigative offices (guide for judges, folders for investigative files, registers, pieces of office furniture, judiciary works). (Sources: Studies carried out by Program of the United Nations for Development, Bureau for the Latin America and the Caribbean - JUSTICE IN HAITI - Report October 1999, pp. 25-26).

Today, the international community has slowed down its efforts of support for the operation of the Haitian judicial system, it thus comes back to the State to continue these various projects in order to reinforce the provision of justice. For this reason, one must greet the project of setting up the appeals court of Port-au-Prince in a new room on Avenue John Brown (Lalue), as well as renovation works on the courthouse in order to give to each investigative magistrate a study.

[66] It is quite regrettable to note that in a good number of our courts file management continues to be done with loose-leaf folders.

It falls back on the Haitian State to continue the work of the setting up of management systems for the courts, in particular, the system of recording, of word processing and follow-up of the files undertaken by Canada's co-operative support of justice in Haiti. There is a need for computerizing the judiciary apparatus so that certain decisions are not mishandled or mislaid.

b. Reform the Superior Council of Magistrates so that the new institution has jurisdiction over all judicial matters, from judges on the bench to public prosecutors, from recruitment to retirement, including promotions, transfers, disciplinary actions, and determinations of judicial incapacity. The Council must have sound, proper operating procedures and direct and real control over administration of tribunals.[67]

Making the Superior Council of Magistrates the principal body of administration and management over the judicial power fulfills one of the necessary conditions of establishing an independent judiciary.

Thus, it is necessary to:

---

[67] Created in 1920, the Superior Council of the Judiciary is, for the moment, an emanation of the Court of Appeal. Already in 1999, this authority had been the subject of new reflections, in particular, on behalf of the Ministry for Justice and Public Safety which, in the document of general policy worked out by the CPRDJ, considers that, within the framework of the Constitution of 1987, "it becomes possible to create a new Superior Council of the Judiciary" while adding: " The restoration of the Council was to contribute to the reinforcement of the independence of the judiciary by replacing the power of control and disciplinary actions within the very center of the institution" (page 41).

It thus becomes necessary to set up this new Superior Council of the Judiciary in order to ensure a clear separation between the judiciary and executive branches, and giving it, within the framework envisaged by the Constitution, the functions of selection, formation and discipline of sitting judges and the police judicial authorities. As important as the very existence of the Superior Council of the Judges detached from the executive power is its makeup. Indeed, it would be efficient that the Council include a representation of all the levels of the judiciary while showing opening towards civil society that could, as certain experiences have shown, also form a part of it.

N.B. One of the two bills ratified by the senators on August 9, 2007 on the reform of justice envisages the creation of the Superior council of the Judiciary, "the body of administration, discipline and deliberation of this power." One of the main missions of the eight members of this Council is to formulate "an opinion concerning the nominations of sitting magistrates and updates the schedule of annual promotions of all magistrates." This Council that will have to be made up, inter alia, of the president of the Supreme Court, of a judge of the Supreme Court, of someone from civil society and a president of a bar association, has a general power of information and recommendation on the state of the judiciary.

c. Develop a new organic framework for the Ministry of Justice that eliminates its powers of intervention and control relative to the judicial power.[68]

---

[68] The decree of March 30, 1984 enacting revision of the basic law of the Ministry of Justice provides that the Ministry of Justice be placed under the authority of a Minister, and has specific powers to organize judiciary institution, to control the activities of the Courts, Courts and Police Headquarters, and the operation of the ministerial offices. According to the decree, the Central administration of the Ministry includes the Head office, the Administrative office and the Management of the Judiciary affairs. The management is divided into services and the services into sections. Rules of procedure define the objectives, the responsibilities and the tasks of the various Directorates and the various Departments.

"The institutional role of the Ministry of Justice and Public Safety is not easy to manage. The Ministry is often perceived as the political official of all judiciary affairs. It is taken hostage by a Jacobin and centralizing logic but without corresponding powers in fact (see decree of March 30, 1984).

The support from international cooperation - with some exceptions is, in general, based, without many results, on the hope of finding in the Ministry Of Justice and Public Safety the institution that would ensure the leadership that is considered necessary. However, this strategy has proven to be inadequate in theory and relatively not very effective in fact, because to build a judicial power independent of the executive power supposes, as a prerequisite, that the executive relinquishes its prerogatives. Moreover, international assistance neglected the other agents of the system of justice and, by doing this, reinforced the executive as the only and single interlocutor as regards the reform of justice.

The Ministry of Justice and Public safety remains nevertheless an unavoidable and decisive agent. Indeed, it is, inter alia, the one in charge of the administration of the courts and the judicial police. Moreover, it is in charge of the good performance of the police force and the prisons.

It is here that the importance of the stakes appears. The reinforcement of an independent judicial power depends as much on a clear separation between the executive and the judiciary powers as that of a good administration of the courts, appeals courts and prisons. Any project that aims at supporting the Superior Council of the Judiciary or the Superior Council of the Higher Authority must aim at the modernization and the improvement of administration to render the exercise of more effective justice.

"...To support the Ministry for Justice and Public safety not strengthening in and for itself its own structure of rendering justice, but to more effectively play its part in listening to the requests for justice, to gradually integrate them into its behaviors and its own structure." (7, Program Project profile of the United Nations for the Development, Office for the Latin America and the Caribbean - JUSTICE IN HAITI - Report October 1999, p. 99).

d. Reform the Supreme Court by refocusing it on its juridical functions.

e. Make the Superior Council of Magistrates the judicial power's budget management body. [69]

f. Develop a new organic framework for the Superior Council of Magistrates' expanded role.

g. Prepare and pass a law concerning the structure of the School for Magistrates by specifying admission criteria for applicants and minimum qualifications for instructors, and by extending the school's training courses to clerks and bailiffs.

h. Develop and approve a Judicial Code of Ethics.

3. Long-Term Reforms

a. Amend the Constitution to revise the general status of Judges. [70]

---

[69] The budget allotted to justice is not managed in an autonomous manner by the judicial system, but directly by the Ministry Of Justice charged according to the decree of 1995 amending the law of September 18, 1985 of the administration of justice.

At the level of the budget, it is necessary for judiciary power to be autonomous. Management of the courts should not come under the Ministry for Justice but under an administrative entity controlled by the Superior Council of the Judiciary or the Superior Council of the Judicial Power.

[70] Considering articles 175,176, and 177 of the Constitution of March 29, 1987 defining the judicial power, justice is clearly under the influence of the executive in particular with regard to the question of the nomination of judges.

On this subject, a technician in judiciary administration, Jumelle Michèle César, writes extremely well to the point in an analysis: "It is astonishing to note that the legislators of 1987 were not able to get rid of the weight of a certain habit of thought which inevitably puts judicial power with the executive, the role given to the Senate of the Republic and the Territorial Collectivities in the designation procedure of the magistrates finding its result only in the final decision, the supreme and unilateral of nomination of President of the Republic." (Jumelle, Michele César, the reform of Haitian Justice in the Judiciary Review of Quisqueya University, Vol. II No January 1 - June 2000).

LEGAL GUARANTEES FOR DEFENDANTS

1. Short-Term Reforms

a. Reinforce and make operational legislation on legal aid;

b. Modernize the decree of September 27, 1985 on criminal penalties;

c. Establish a nationwide program of sensitization and legal education for the general public;

d. Organize training seminars on the execution of judicial decisions for officers of the Prosecutor's Office, Appeals judges (judges of "*référés*", or provisional rulings in urgent cases), court officers and police officers.

2. Medium-term reforms

a. Reform the legal profession by instituting new conditions of access to the profession and new requirements for admission to the bar.
b. Repeal the law of June 6, 1919, as modified by the laws of June 29, 1942 and July 14, 1952 regulating lawyers' guilds and bachelors of law.

c. Create the institution of grand jury magistrates to speed up judicial proceedings.

d. Create the institution of sentencing judges to fill the gaps of the decree of June 5, 1995 on the APENA.

e. Reform the handling of disputed claims to facilitate access to administrative justice and overhaul appeal procedures in administrative and financial matters.

f. Reform the Supreme Court of the Republic as well as the Appeals Courts by organizing them into specialized judicial chambers or sections.

3. Long-Term Reforms

a. Augment the system's jurisdictional reach by the creation of new tribunals.[71]

---

[71] The judiciary organization of Haiti has its origins in the Napoleonic judiciary setup and has preserved several aspects to date from it. The Constitution of the Republic of Haiti of March 29, 1987, the order in Council of August 22, 1995 amending the law of September 18, 1985 relating to judiciary organization and the law on judiciary reform of May 8, 1998, are the principal recent texts which condition the organization of the judiciary apparatus and the administration of justice in Haiti. The Haitian Judiciary Body consists approximately of 650 magistrates.

The main agents of the judicial system are the judges, the government commissioners and substitutes, the clerks and ushers who constitute the Judiciary corps.

The Haitian judiciary apparatus consists of the Courts of Peace, the County courts, the Appeal Courts, the Supreme Court and of the Special courts. The Court of Peace represents the bottom level of the judicial hierarchy. It is charged with regulating matters of little value. There exist approximately 185 Courts of Peace through the country.

Article 81 of the decree of August 22, 1995 specifies that there be at least a Court of Peace in each commune and each one is made up of a judge, of a substitute and a clerk.

The County court has full jurisdiction, that is to say, that it is qualified to handle all the civil commercial and maritime cases, since a special law does not allow the Special court to handle them.

There exist eighteen (18) County courts spread over ten (10) departments: Port-au-Prince, Cape-Haitian, Cayes, Gonaïves, Small-Goâve, Jacmel, Saint-Marc, Aquin, Fort-Liberté, Hinche, Mirebalais, Grand-Rivière du Nord, Anse-A-Veau, Jérémie, Port-de Paix, Miragoâne, Croix DesBouquets, Coteaux.

The Courts of Appeal constitute a jurisdiction of Common Law and of second degree. They rule on fact and the law. They can hear civil, criminal and commercial cases.

There exist five (5) Courts of Appeal in the country. Their seats are in Port-au-Prince, Cape-Haitian, Gonaïves, Cayes, Hinche. A Court of Appeal installed with the Law courts of Port-au-Prince plays the part of Supreme Court of the country. It is charged with taking care of the strict observation of the law.

Given the number of Courts for the whole country estimated at nearly 8.5 million inhabitants, it has to be recognized that formal justice is not known in a way structural by more of two thirds of the population.

Indeed, there does not exist currently any presence of an unspecified judiciary apparatus on the level of the basic territorial subdivision that is the communal

b. Reform civil statutes to facilitate determination of the identification of citizens before tribunals.[72]

c. Organize citizens' records.[73]

d. Modernize and simplify judicial procedures in civil, penal, commercial and administrative matters by revising codes.[74]

---

section. Consequently, it becomes urgent that the State increase the jurisdictional cover of the territory by the creation of new courts in order to answer citizens' demand for justice. (See study project of the Ministry of Justice within the framework of the activation of a project of itinerant justice).

[72] Civil services being practically the first and often the only services rendered by the State with each citizen taken individually, no relationship of confidence can be established in a lasting way between the two protagonists as long as the State will not provide tangible proof of its will to recognize everyone as a full citizen.

The request for recognition of status and therefore of citizen rights is at the base of any restoration. The State must thus guarantee a common status of citizenship for all the population. For that, it is necessary to arrive as fast as possible at the restoration of the Civil State. If it is true that the State sets about the process of its own transformation by extending itself to the whole national community, it remains that it is identified as an institution of service provider. It is indeed a question for it of assuming through its administration a mission of socio-cultural integration that cannot avoid the precondition of the recognition of the citizenship. The search for more close integration thus implies an effort of involvement, at a local level, of all of the members of society for the launching of a true reinforcement campaign of the Civil State. In other words, integration of citizens must take the form of a mobilizing process. The process of the constitution of citizenship through which one becomes eligible for rights succeeds by involving all the members of the community on a local and decentralized basis. (See in Justice in Haiti, the subtitle: a failing civil status for 40% of the population. Report published in October 1999, page 33, by the mission of The United Nations for the Development, Project for the Latin America and the Caribbean).

[73] Police records : refers to the project of setting up of a scientific analysis laboratory in Port-au-Prince.

[74] Noting that reform projects are under development, it is noteworthy that the majority of the new texts, particularly the law on the Superior Council of the Judicial Power, were adopted without dialogue, without an impact study and without any significant means for considering its implementation.

It is worrisome that urgency and media pressure usually bring about the adoption of the reforms. However, any reform without collective reflection and consensus is likely to appear illegitimate and, because of this, ineffective.

e. Reorganize the judicial system by adopting either a juridically dualist or juridically monistic model.[75]

Illegitimate because just the agreement of the Government and of Parliament is not enough unfortunately to be able to affirm a level of sufficient consensus has been reached. The absence of reflection and consensus is also likely to make ineffective the concrete actions to be undertaken because the reform of justice must follow a complex way where, even if several agents end up engaging, others can create obstacles to it.

It is in this context that one can regard as essential the creation of a National Commission of Reform of Justice, preferably situated at the presidential level, and whose main mission must be to generate this consensus in the field of justice reform. It must simultaneously therefore make it possible to express the interests of all the agents, to guarantee an effective and constructive participation of the latter and, finally, to be carried out in a place of dialogue.

This process not only makes it possible to recognize the existence and the role of the various agents of justice but especially to make the way of developing the code and law an exemplary process of the renewal of the democratic game. The Commission should thus control the design of the whole of the reform.

One must, beginning with the work already completed by the preparatory Commission with the Reform of Justice and the governmental action plan (PAG) of May 1999, set up this Commission of reform charged with bringing the codes and the laws up to date. The reorganization of the justice of minors, the rural code, the adaptation of the penal code, the criminal instruction code, the civil code, the code of civil procedure, the labor rules, commercial law, taxation laws etc to the social and economic reality of the country are among the priorities. What is at stake is the modernization of justice in Haiti.

N.B. This project of reforming the codes and laws should not ignore the existence of common law. In short, Haitian leaders would have to think of working out a plan of reform of our judicial system conformant with our historical cultural and ancestral values.

[75] The Rule of Law prevails where the Government itself is held to respect the law, all the members of society are treated in the same way according to the law; the dignity of each individual is recognized and protected by the law and justice is accessible to all. Consequently, the Rule of Law requires an independent judicial system in which the courts can interpret and apply the laws and regulations in an impartial, foreseeable, effective and transparent way. The application of the law ensures in its turn a stable institutional climate in which the long-term consequences of economic decisions can be evaluated.

REINFORCING THE RULE OF LAW

In Haiti we have not learned respect for the law. The Constitution and the law are referenced only to justify often-illegal pronouncements or rulings. Our society is based on personalities (political or economic), not on laws and institutions. And yet under the Rule of Law, authority can only exists in terms of the law. Under the Rule of Law, only the law can grant power and authority.[76]

Indeed, the greatest obstacle to judicial reform is making laws and dedicating ourselves to respecting them. Respect for the law is the one indispensable condition of reform. Only respect for the law will make it possible for justice to occupy its rightful place and will lead us toward establishment of a society based on the Rule of Law.[77]

Two important issues must considered to reinforce the Rule of Law in Haiti: public safety and justice.

---

[76] "The Government pays special attention to the implementation of the reform of the justice without which a Rule of Law will never be born in Haiti. It will also insist on the implementation of the reform of the public office, the guarantor of a good administrative State. " (Prime Minister Jacques Edouard Alexis, Declaration of Policy General, June 2006, p. 4).

N.B. Without a fundamental reform of the judicial system, one cannot guarantee the respect for human rights, and the Rule of Law will remain a Utopia.

[77] See various legislation related to the principle of the protection of Human rights in force in Haiti: Haitian constitution of March 29, 1987 ED. Henri Deschamps, P.au.P., March 1993,211 pages. (Monitor of April 281987 #36). Universal Declaration of Human rights (adopted by the General Assembly of the United Nations in its resolution 217 has (III) of December 10, 1948).

International Pact Relative to Civil and Political laws adopted on December 16, 1966, came into effect on March 23, 1976. American Convention Relative to Human rights or Pact of San Jose of Costa Rica of November 22, 1969, came into effect on July 18, 1978. Code of Conduct for the Project Manager of the Laws (The United Nations December 17, 1979 resolution 34/169).

Decree of September 12, 1995 creating an office called: Office of Protection of the Citizen and the Citizen (Monitor of Monday October 16 1995 #82 A).

1. Ensuring Public Safety:

a. Undertake in-depth, non-partisan reform that takes into account the aspirations of the Haitian people.

b. Establish judicial structures (among the judiciary and among police forces) that serve the best interests of the people.

c. Guarantee the individual safety of all defendants.

d. Carry out of a national disarmament plan.

At this level, we formulate the following proposals:

2. Ensuring Justice

a. Monitor the quality of justice.

b. Ensure judicial independence (reasonable wages, career and job security) for the civil servants of justice.

c. Educate people, and inform defendants of their legal rights and duties.

d. Convince defendants of the judicial system's effectiveness and promote the proposed changes.

e. Ensure adequate training of judges.

f. Redesign civil codes and laws.

g. Establish uniform procedures in each field.

h. Reinforce the strength of the Judicial Investigation Department.

i. Make jurisprudential and legal information available to judges and to the public by means of seminars, conferences, debates, and via radio and television.

j. Penalize all acts of impunity, arbitrariness, abuses of power and corruption by members of the judiciary, the police and their accomplices.[78]

---

[78] With regard to the function of the maintenance of order of the institution of police people arrested are held in a police station or a sub police station after their arrest. Under the terms of Haitian legislation, this detention should not

k. Solve the crucial problem of arbitrary and prolonged detentions.[79]

---

exceed forty-eight hours before the prisoner is transferred to a civil prison (Article 26 of the Constitution); however in the reality of things, the person can be kept for several days in the cells of the police stations.

In Haiti, these people placed in detention in these police stations are in cells with reduced dimensions, deprived of elementary and necessary facilities such as: beds, ventilators, toilets. The defendants must use "pots" which often stay for hours and even days before being emptied.

Moreover it should be emphasized that the citizens in detention are victims of abnormal behaviors of the members of the police force who mistreat them by walking all over their basic rights. A provisional examination of the detention conditions clearly reveals the dysfunction of the Haitian judiciary apparatus. The majority of prisoners are awaiting judgment. Some even have never met a judge since their imprisonment. The illegality of detention, its unlimited duration and the uncertainty of the accused about their fate worsen the difficulties of imprisonment. The high number of prisoners contributes to the deterioration of their physical and psychological conditions. Sometimes, the prisoners are piled up in cells where it is impossible for them to lie down. They must adapt to a new and often dangerous environment. Overpopulation and dirtiness facilitate the transmission of infectious illness. Article 9-3 of the international Pact relating to civil laws and policies states that detention pending trial should not be the rule but the exception. Also regarding the abuses of rights documented against the person of the prisoners, it is important that concrete actions are considered for solving the thorn problem of arbitrary and prolonged detention.

[79] With regard to the function of the maintenance of order of the institution of police people arrested are held in a police station or a sub police station after their arrest. Under the terms of Haitian legislation, this detention should not exceed forty-eight hours before the prisoner is transferred to a civil prison (Article 26 of the Constitution); however in the reality of things, the person can be kept for several days in the cells of the police stations.

In Haiti, these people placed in detention in these police stations are in cells with reduced dimensions, deprived of elementary and necessary facilities such as: beds, ventilators, toilets. The defendants must use "pots" which often stay for hours and even days before being emptied.

Moreover it should be emphasized that the citizens in detention are victims of abnormal behaviors of the members of the police force who mistreat them by walking all over their basic rights. A provisional examination of the detention conditions clearly reveals the dysfunction of the Haitian judiciary apparatus. The majority of prisoners are awaiting judgment. Some even have never met a judge since their imprisonment. The illegality of detention, its unlimited

3. The Problem of Lawlessness

Lawlessness is more and more a crucial problem in Haiti. It appears in the form of acts of violence such as political assassination, attacks, armed robberies, vandalism, torture, extortion, and kidnapping. According to studies and firsthand investigations, the factors influencing insecurity are the following:

a. A nonfunctional justice system;

b. The existence of numerous, highly active criminal gangs;

c. The emergence of groups of deportees coming from the United States of America;

d. The massive circulation of illegal weapons;

e. The existence of judicial double standards;

f. The abuse of rights;

g. Political instability;

h. Corruption;

i. A lack of confidence in the judicial system;

j. Repeated violations of human rights;

k. The illicit drug trade; and

l. Socio-economic problems;

---

duration and the uncertainty of the accused about their fate worsen the difficulties of imprisonment. The high number of prisoners contributes to the deterioration of their physical and psychological conditions. Sometimes, the prisoners are piled up in cells where it is impossible for them to lie down. They must adapt to a new and often dangerous environment. Overpopulation and dirtiness facilitate the transmission of infectious illness. Article 9-3 of the international Pact relating to civil laws and policies states that detention pending trial should not be the rule but the exception. Also regarding the abuses of rights documented against the person of the prisoners, it is important that concrete actions are considered for solving the thorn problem of arbitrary and prolonged detention.

4. Proposals for Eliminating Lawlessness

a. Organize targeted sectors and set up neighborhood safety systems to better target the authors of crimes;

b. Implement a program of sensitization, information, accountability, and mobilization;

c. Inculcate the concepts of community policing with the national police force;

d. Develop a program of reintegration to the workforce for former servicemen and deportees in the fields of the environment, construction, road-building and communications infrastructure; and

e. Establish an effective internal and external communication system allowing rapid execution and dissemination of judicial rulings.

5. Police Reform

a. Set up of an infrastructure of judicial monitoring of the police;[80]

---

[80] The Haitian police force made considerable efforts to train its personnel, to spread themselves - particularly in the urban zones in a country with difficult means of communication - to engage in the organization of special operational services, to set up an acceptable administration and, finally, to set the way for internal control through the Inspector General.

All the commentators agree that the police force is practically the only institution having achieved serious progress during the last several years. In any event, it is always insulated in the Haitian institutional context. Indeed, the step consisting of strengthening the organization of the police force without conceiving of it as being part of the system of administration of justice as a whole, and without at the same time strengthening the judiciary apparatus with – at least - the same means, leads to the inability of the judicial system to control the legality of the activity of the police force (of detention, investigation, etc). Strengthening of the police force in isolation reaffirms the social perception of the State as a potentially violent structure and exposes this new institution with a renewal of the traditional mistrust of the people towards the official institutions.

These above mentioned reasons confirm the idea that the reform, or rather, in the case of Haiti, the creation of the police force, should not be conceived as a problem isolated from the remainder of the institutional chart, but which must belong to a general strategy of transformation of the system of justice. It is

b. Ensure adequate training of police officers;

c. Make police officers accountable;

d. Facilitate understanding and communication between the police force and citizens;[81]

e. Establish a prevention program;

f. Change the police force's negative image;

g. Use schools and the media to inform the public of the role of the police force in service to the people;[82]

h. Establish the credibility of the police force while penalizing abuses of power or authority;[83]

---

desirable to consider an innovative approach of the reform of this sector, in order to rebalance the institutional framework and to avoid involuntary drifting.

Also, it is necessary to strengthen the principle of judicial control to prevent or to punish the human rights abuses of citizens by the police. Let us recall that the Constitution of 1987 lays out in article 274 that: "the members of the police force in the performance of their duties are subject to civil and criminal law." The same principle is taken again by article 29 of the code of discipline of the PNH.

[81] The new police force was set up urgently, under the strong pressure of the international community and because of the government's haste to fill the institutional vacuum caused by disappearance of the army. It is undoubtedly for this reason that public debate in this regard did not take place and that the current police organization has not yet established a true communication with the people. Which model of police force for Haiti and the Haitians? The question always remains timely.

[82] Reference to the importance of the civic education campaign to inform the public of the role of the police force in the service of the people.

[83] If it is true that many things improved with the presence of the new director Mario Andrésol as the head of the HNP, it is no less true that mistreatments inflicted by police officers remain still too numerous. In practice and according to tradition, the police officer always acts as if he was above the law and in any case for the most part, above the justice system on which, however, is blamed for this impunity. The reports of investigations carried out often tend to justify the police action and to clear the police officers of the charges by the people. The sanction against some agents for the abuses committed -rarely is the case- is treated in most cases, however, by the police force as an internal affair.

Of all these considerations, it is essential that the State begin to strengthen its means of action so that these arbitrary and daily practices do not keep happening any longer. The Haitian State must begin under the direction of the Inspector

i. Establish a safety commission to watch over public safety; and

j. Create an Ethics Commission that contains members of civil society to monitor police behavior.[84]

6. Human Rights

Reinforcing the Rule of Law is one of the most serious concerns in Haiti.[85] In reality, in spite of the presence of the Mission of the United Nations for Stabilization in Haiti peacekeeping force (MINUSTAH), Haiti remains plunged in an ongoing human rights crisis.

In spite of a more conscientious approach to the issue, many arbitrary acts continue to be committed and perpetrators continue to circulate with complete impunity. Poor treatment, extrajudicial executions, the deliberate and arbitrary murder of civilians, rapes, death threats and acts of kidnapping remain standard fare, and victims seldom have the luxury of police and legal protection. Violence has been aggravated by the proliferation of weapons. Disarmament thus has become the most central issue the government must tackle to arrive at a solution.[86]

General of the National police force (IGPN) so that fast and effective investigations include the apprehension of police officers guilty of violations of human rights. In order for the people to trust the will or ability of the State to sanction abuses, it is important to make the results of the sanctions public.

[84] An organized civil society can give its support in the fight against the acts that violate civil rights. While engaging actively, this organized civil society can become a body for denouncing abuse on a national as well as international scale. All in all, this civil society will be a real societal protector in order to defeat the arbitrary acts of the agents of the state .

[85] Several studies were carried out on the reinforcement of the Rule of Law in Haiti. See in the Bibliography the list of the conferences, of reports, of the works written on the question.

[86] The latest reports and statistics give a report on clear improvement in the field with respect to human rights in Haiti. The question of restoring safety was a first battle won by the current government. Indeed, the redevelopment project of Police Department of Port-au-Prince placed in a room renovated on John Brown Avenue and the reinforcement of the ability of the police force to operate, especially in the metropolitan zones of Port-au-Prince, are signs of encouragement.

JUSTICE AND HUMAN RIGHTS

Within the framework of judicial reform, the government must:

a. Condemn all attacks on human rights and express its total opposition to these acts; make it clearly known to all governmental and nongovernmental agents that human rights infringements will not be tolerated under any circumstances; demonstrate its will to make human rights respected in Haiti; and cooperate with the international community to achieve such respect;[87]

b. Immediately take effective measures to develop, implement and supervise an exhaustive and lasting disarmament, demobilization and reintegration (DDR) program. At each step, take advantage of the assistance and expertise of the international community. Apply the DDR program neutrally to armed groups and to all civilians with weapons. Create an independent commission made up of representatives of civil society, including representatives of the media, to inspect and monitor the DDR process, and regularly inform the public of its progress.

c. Put an end to arbitrary arrests and take effective measures to end to the generalized practice of arbitrary detention.[88]

---

[87] See the presidential decree of February 3, 2005 of the government Boniface/Latortue creating the National Commission of disarmament.

N.B. The research undertaken in 2004 and 2005 by the program on Small Arms Survey, based in Geneva, shows that, in Haiti, about 170.000 weapons are in the hands of private individuals, various armed groups and criminal bands, security services and the officers of the law. According to the report of the Small Arms Survey, there does not exist to date a complete, precise, and up to date file on firearms; there used to be a national registry, but it was abandoned although gun licenses were granted at the beginning of 2005. The official figures given in the report indicate that, in 2001, the national police force had recorded 20,300 weapons held legally by civilians.

[88] The respect for basic rights constitutes an ideal to which nations, governments, aspire. But, history shows that these rights are not ever acquired once and for all; and that there have often been advances and retreats in this field by societies. Haiti obtained a tool leading towards an ideal within the framework of human rights with the Constitution of March 29, 1987, which is, after all, the judiciary document of the highest value. This Constitution installs the obligations for the government as well as for the governed, and whose respect must be immediate and unquestioned.

d. Guarantee fair trials as soon as possible to all prisoners, with complete respect for their rights to a defense, in particular the right of appeal to a higher, independent judicial body.[89]

However, violations of human rights occur from time to time. The overzealousness of the persons in charge of certain institutions, the tendency of certain individuals, their concept of authority, often leads them to want to step all over the basic rights of citizens by arbitrary acts contrary to constitutional provisions. In this respect, even the judicial system, the competent authority for repressing these acts and for bringing help to the victims appears inept to stop these violations.

It is thus duty of the State to reinforce the justice system to take hold of the authors of the violations and thus to show its will to make Human rights to be respected.

[89] Article 24-3 of the Constitution concerning the freedom of an individual states clearly that: "The responsibility is personal. No one can be arrested in the place of another." This principle is a constitutional matter but in Haitian reality, the strict respect of the spirit and the letter of the Constitution are not taken into account.

By seeking an individual suspected of having committed an infringement punished by the law, those who carry out arbitrary acts always tend to arrest, without judiciary authorization, an influential member of the family, a close friend until the one suspected decides to turn himself in.

The State must intervene vigorously to put an end to arbitrary arrests and to take effective measures to put an end to the practice of preventive detention. Thus, the following guarantees must be applied:

a. All detentions must be recorded and controlled.

b. The prisoners must be presented quickly to a judge - Haitian constitution of 1987 requires that prisoners must be heard by a judge within forty-eight hours of their arrest or released.

c. Prisoners must have the possibility of consulting a lawyer and a doctor of their choice at the time of their arrest.

d. All prisoners must have the possibility of disputing the illegality of their detention.

e. Judges must make sure that prisoners are not tortured or maltreated and must do follow-up investigations in the event of torture or of alleged bad treatment.

f. It is necessary to set up a system of investigations that are regular, independent, and without any restriction, of all the places of detention, including prisons placed under the auspices of the Administration of the National Penitentiary (APENA) and of the police stations.

e. Take immediate measures to prevent extrajudicial executions, in accordance with United Nations principles relating to effective prevention of extrajudicial arbitrary and summary executions, and supply the means to investigate these executions.[90]

e. Take immediate measures to put an end to torture and mistreatment, including the lack of medical care for prisoners and life-threatening detention conditions.

f. All complaints and information alleging human rights violations must be the object, as soon as possible, of an impartial and effective inquiry carried out by a body independent from the officials in question, and possessing sufficient authority and means to do so. The methods and conclusions of all investigations must be made public. Plaintiffs, witnesses and other threatened people must be protected from all intimidations and all reprisals.

g. The persons responsible for human rights violations must be brought to justice. This principle must apply to all presumed authors of such acts, no matter the length of time that has passed since the crime. Lawsuits must be equitable and in conformity with international standards. Persons responsible for these acts should not be permitted to take advantage of legal measures allowing them to escape legal proceedings or judgments.

h. Take care that prohibitions against torture, extrajudicial executions and other human rights violations are integrated into the training of all persons charged with administering justice - judges, police officers, and prison wardens. Such training must be

---

These visits could be carried out by non-governmental organizations, which were to be authorized to go into all the places of detention without restriction.

[90] To fight extrajudicial executions, the State must:

a. Condemn publicly and vigorously extra-judicial executions;

b. Explicitly prohibit these infringements of the law and take care that they are punished by suitable penalties taking into account the gravity of the crime;

c. Take care that law enforcement officers use force only when it is strictly necessary and only in the measure required by the circumstances; deadly force should not be used except in the event of peremptory necessity protecting the life;

d. Take care that those in charge of security forces exert a strict oversight so that agents placed under their command do not carry out extrajudicial executions.

based on international standards relative to treatment of prisoners and for the use of firearms by those responsible for upholding laws, in particular United Nations standards.[91]

i. Give the victims of human rights violations and their heirs equitable and sufficient reparations from the State, in particular in the form of financial compensation.[92]

j. Contribute to rebuilding and reinforcing the legal and judicial system.[93]

Recent political events have seriously weakened the Haitian judicial system. The School for Magistrates, the only specialized judicial training body, has ceased its training program. However, protecting human rights over the long term requires the existence of an effective, independent, impartial and accessible judicial system, and a judiciary with the means to accomplish its mandate.

The international community must help the Haitian government to rebuild an effective judicial system and a competent judiciary. However, initiatives in this field must be accompanied by a determination on the part of the State to bring to justice persons responsible for human rights violations.

---

[91] Training Sessions in Human Right for the agents of various public office at the national level should be organized. The restructured School of Judges could host these meetings.

[92] See article 27-1 of the Haitian Constitution of March 29, 1987 on the civil and criminal responsibilities of the Government officials.

[93] The thought here is that the reform of Justice in Haiti cannot be conceived apart from the reform of the State. For a real reform of justice in Haiti, one must go towards the very reorganization of the Haitian State. "The modernization of the State, one of the showpieces of Government action, comprises three dimensions: the restructuring of the State, the support for the consolidation of democratic institutions, and the deployment of the State apparatus throughout the entire national territory. These will contribute to the politico-institutional standardization and introduction of a new State." (Haitian the Prime Minister Jacques Edouard Alexis, Declaration of General policy, June 2006, p.4)

JUDICIAL REFORM BEGINS WITH ESTABLISHING THE RULE OF LAW

The Rule of Law also presumes taking into account basic human rights: the right to the life, health, work, housing, food, education and safety. The government must increase its efforts in the battle against poverty. It must promote changes in the governance of the State to make public administration, the judicial apparatus and public services more efficient, more responsive and more accountable to its citizens. The administration should be decentralized, and decisions also should be decentralized to bring institutions closer to their constituents. The government must urgently devise a strategy to reduce poverty by offering more opportunities to impoverished citizens. That means increasing employment, granting credit, building roads, providing electricity, running water, decent sanitary conditions, adequate housing, decent schools, proper health care and most importantly, providing adequate safety for all citizens.[94]

---

[94] "... The fourth condition, and not least, is that which Haitian men and women cry out for today with the most insistence. They want the State to takes responsibility for ensuring safety and maintenance of law and order as well as the protection of people and goods: in a word, they want the authority of the State to be restored, the Government to carry out a fight at every moment against all forms of criminality, and to be committed to significantly reducing insecurity in our cities and our society by improving the presence of our police forces throughout the national territory, and by facilitating the implementation of a real program of disarmament, mobilization and reintegration. It remains understood, in addition, that safety cannot be effective, nor lasting without a real rise in the standard of living and a better access to an equitable justice." (Prime Minister Jacques Edouard Alexis, Declaration of General policy, June 2006).

CHAPTER IV:
JUDICIAL REFORM IN HAITI: A CHALLENGE TO BE OVERCOME

The absence of moral values in the Haitian community has deeply affected the justice system. The judiciary has evolved under the influence of poorly suited laws and has suffered from Magistrates who lack all moral virtue. Dignity, fairness, individual responsibility, and respect for human rights constitute the moral prerequisites for the distribution of justice. Competence and honesty should be the minimum requirements in selecting judges.

Within the framework of a Haitian judicial reform, the first step should be to improve working conditions by supplying the judiciary with adequate material resources and truly qualified human resources.

The same problems have persisted for many years and the urgency remains the same: inadequate pay, material and technical problems, the lack of computerization in clerks' offices, no judicial specialization, outdated and obsolete codes and laws, and finally, the sometimes catastrophically dire state of decay of court buildings, tribunals and police stations. To establish the Rule of Law in Haiti, in-depth reform of the judicial system is a necessity.

An action plan for reform should contain the following items:

a. Create a specialized body to combat financial fraud, to prevent and punish the corruption that corrodes the highest levels of government, public and private enterprises, and saps the legitimacy of the State authority in the face of delinquency the lawlessness.[95]

---

[95] Our study finds that the Haitian judicial system is not able to pursue, to investigate and judge financial crimes under good conditions. In the rarified affairs of financial crimes, the accused, that is, society at large, is in a state of inferiority vis-à-vis the battalions of lawyers of a business, vis-à-vis the expert public accountants: the Police station allows substitute prosecutors, all by

b. Reorganize the Haitian government to ensure the implementation of recommended reforms.[96]

c. Create a citizen's National Public Service organization managed by an inter-ministerial committee.

Without the political will to make the changes that guarantee each citizen's constitutional rights, the State will inevitably sink beneath the combined flood of financial crime, removing the last defenses against brutality and harm from smuggling, armed gangs, and the anarchy of an atrophied banking system that drowns

---

themselves, who sometimes haven't even followed the investigation. The weakness of so many of the experts and judicial assistants does not make it possible for justice in financial matters to function quickly and effectively: the magistrates and investigative services are deprived of the most essential means to fulfill their functions.

Faced with this vacuum, it is recommended to fill the needs for training of the professionals of justice while also advocating for the improvement of the transparency of the financial circles. The current situation supports impunity and undermines economic law and order and involves a great inequality of citizens before the law.

In this respect, we need:

- to manage the problem of competence of the magistrates on economic questions;

- an administration of justice able to answer in a reasonable time to the cases which it is given;

- means for a modernized management of financial investigations.

It is necessary to reinforce the capacity of national institutions among which are the Superior court of Accounts and Administrative Dispute (CSC/CA), the Central Processing Unit of Financial Information (UCREF), the General Financial Investigation Unit (IGF), the Unit of the Fight Against Corruption (ULCC) and National Commission of Government Contracts (CNMP).

[96] See the law of September 6, 1982 defining the national public administration. (Monitor of October 28, 1982 #75) and the law of September 19, 1982 establishing the general status of the Haitian public office (Monitor of November 11, 1982 #78). See Haitian Constitution of 1987, chapter of the Public administration.

legitimate businesses.[97] The Government must invest adequate funds to manage judicial reform, the first step towards the modernization of the State. [98]

To achieve modernization, the government should:

a. Recruit and train thirty thousand new judicial and police force employees;

---

[97] The reform of the judicial power is essential to face the phenomena of globalization and integration of the worldwide economy. In this period of deep changes, the judiciary order is essential. For example, one of the challenges with which countries in the process of development are confronted is the installation of a modern and effective judicial system, likely to support the blossoming of an atmosphere of safety and confidence for all their citizens. Haiti is no exception to the rule.

Without an effective judicial system, without clear and precise laws, flexible support of the growth of economic activities and financial procedures, the development of the country will be only Utopian. Moreover, the decisions of investment are made, nowadays, on the basis of economic consideration. The investors want to make sure that the country has an independent judicial power, that it is law and not arbitrariness that governs social and economic relations.

Moreover, the modernization of the judicial system aims at satisfying the principal demands of the people. It's a matter, of course, of establishing a system guaranteeing the distribution of a healthy, objective, impartial and timely justice. Only an independent judicial power and an autonomous judiciary administration can promote such a justice. (See Problems of Judiciary Reform in Haiti. Philippe Vixamar, March 1996).

[98] Read the Declaration of General Policy of Prime Minister Jacques Edouard Alexis on the Modernization of the State, June 2006, p. 4: "

The construction of a modern country involves the modernization of the State itself. This transformation will make our State:

•   A strategic State i.e. a State able to effectively play its normative role of direction and encouragement of economic and social development of the nation and to provide services essential to its citizens.

•   A decentralized State in which Territorial collectivities will be able to play an active role in the development their respective areas.

•   A Rule of Law which ensures at all times and in all circumstances compliance with the Rule of Law and protection of citizens, men and women, without discrimination, from all forms of arbitrariness.

•   A State well administered which will apply public policies with rigor, effectiveness and efficiency."

b. Allocate funds for the re-organizational and operational needs of the judiciary and the police force;

c. Allocate funds for building construction, court equipment, prosecutors' offices, police stations and penitentiaries;

d. Augment civil servant salaries;

e. Provide for life insurance and mortgage security proportional to individual wages after eighteen months on the job for public safety and judicial employees;

f. Equip the judiciary with qualified, just and courageous men;[99]

g. Reinforce investigative services in the Ministry of Justice and in police force;

h. Establish a Judicial Reform Commission with a focus on solving long-term problems;[100]

---

[99] The creation of a School for Judges in Haiti (EMMA) in 1996 gave rise to a core of young, qualified and courageous magistrates determined to carry out the battle for the change of the Haitian judiciary apparatus. However, a lack of leadership and the sabotage of the system by certain political "anti-change" authorities almost wiped out the impetus of these professionals.

[100] In the immediate future it is important to start the reform process of justice in Haiti, to seek to see the importance first of all of what has been done taking into account the lessons drawn from the experiences of these last years and putting this strategy into a perspective of the long run. All analyses undertaken concerning the systemic dimension of the problem of justice lead obligatorily to structural changes and must thus be seen from the point of view of the long haul.

On this point, these changes obviously run into the special precariousness of any intervention in the form of a United Nations Mission. The fact that a Mission is generally characterized by its limited time and objectives, defined according to a particular economic situation, makes it unsuitable a priori for supporting long-term programs. Therefore it seems that therein reside some of the causes of the inability of the interventions to obtain results, in particular with regard to strengthening institutions. The nature of the problems to be solved obliges us to seek ways to find a balance between the constraints, dependent on generally short duration and the limited mandate of outside interventions - in particular with regard to a Mission of the United Nations - and long-term objectives, the one condition of a real and durable assumption of responsibility for results.

This fundamental option thus requires setting the work of an intensified strengthening of institutions into an overall strategy defined on the basis of public policy designed for this sector. It remains understood that this cannot be done except from within the framework of a State that carries out strategic choices and tactics, and that integrates the international contribution into its strategy of implementation of national policy. It follows from there that the

i. Restructure the School for Magistrates to make it functional and effective; [101] and,

j. Give the judicial power sound, effective independence. [102]

---

projects must be conceived, set up and evaluated jointly with the local social and institutional agents. International assistance must consequently flow from the model of technical accompaniment and integrate a dynamic wherein all the local agents gather together with the support of the international institutions.

It is necessary to take time for that. As the Economic and Social Council of the United Nations suggests in its report on Haiti (July 1999), it would be preferable to give up the aspect of urgency and rehabilitation for that of the long run and new construction. Just as for the short term we are obliged to work in the existing context with the agents in place, so also, if one gives oneself a ten years' deadline, one must expect to end up with other partners. That assumes obviously a social project that connects with others and not just a simple project of the State. However, such a project cannot exist unless it pulls together with others. It is necessary to take account of the current weakness of the State. For that it is appropriate:

a. not to focus too much on only the institutional - legislative and judiciary - aspects, to solve the difficulties. The risk would be then, either not to succeed, or to lead to legislation destined to remain unapplied;

b. not to overestimate the ability of the State to reform itself;

c. to strengthen it thanks to the support of citizens and the intermediary structures;

d. not to accentuate current imbalances between the institutions themselves: police, judiciary and prison. (See document prepared by the Council Economic and Social of the United Nations over Haiti, July 1999).

[101] Pass the law on the establishment of the School of Judges filed with Parliament.

[102] Judiciary reform ultimately aims at increasing the independence, effectiveness and the equity of the judicial system as well as access to justice; it is imperative that the courts behave with competence and probity on the operational and administrative level so that justice equal for all is a reality everywhere. In Haiti, one must reinforce the judicial power as one of the powers of the State, definitely separate from the executive and legislative powers.

REFLECTIONS FROM COLLEAGUES

The remarks made here come from fellow lawyers, magistrates and human rights activists: Atty. Gerard Gourgue, Jean Vandal, Camille Leblanc, Enerlio Gassant, Stanley Gaston, Antoine O. Vilaire, Eddy Nelson, Gladys Legros, Sabine Butcher, Ketsia Charles, Heidi Fortuné, Renan Hédouville, Henri Dorléans, Jean Marie Robert Paulvin, Andre Michelle Civil, Jean-Claude Bajeux, Jean Lhérisson, Father Jan Hanssens, Juan Gabriel Valdés, Danielle Saada, and Louis Joinet. I must make a point of giving them my sincere thanks for their contribution to this chapter. They have all contributed their thoughts on the problems of justice in Haiti.

Eddy Nelson[103]

Judicial reform in Haiti is closely related to reforming the Haitian mindset. The Magistrate's role and status must be respected. I recommend a true focus on judges in the system.

Gladys Legros[104]

For there to be a Rule of Law in Haiti, private individuals and public authorities, i.e. the State itself, must simultaneously submit to the law. The State must accept the idea that it too is subject to the judicial rulings that result from the laws it has enacted and which it has asked everyone to respect.

Construction of this Rule of Law also presupposes a powerful judicial administration with structures adapted to the country's needs: the fight against impunity and for respect for human dignity.

---

[103] Eddy Nelson is a licensed lawyer with the Bar of Port-au-Prince.

[104] Gladys Legros is a licensed lawyer with the Bar of Port-au-Prince.

Ernélio Gassant[105]

In Haiti, the judiciary functions very poorly and absolutely no transparency exists in carrying out justice. The procedures for nominating and selecting judges make judicial independence impossible. Honestly, I believe that the judiciary must work in the direction of institutional and decisional independence, in order to merit being called a separate power within the Constitutional framework.

Sabine Boucher[106]

In Haiti, the judicial system is dysfunctional for the simple reason that the State does not invest in it. Moreover, justice is politicized. Politicians who make use of it to regulate "their personal and petty businesses" hold it hostage. These gentlemen have the right to name, revoke, or to move judges as they please. Apart from the technical and administrative difficulties, one must also take note of the poor state of the judicial infrastructure. The miserable material conditions that Haitian judicial personnel find themselves in amounts to destruction of the judicial power and the impossibility of applying fair judicial standards.

As a solution to the problems confronted by my country's justice system, I would suggest that one gather together all those involved in the system. All the stakeholders involved must reflect together on the problems of reform in order to formulate a lasting plan that will set the system straight.

Renan Hédouville[107]

Judicial reform in Haiti presupposes awareness on the part of the general population to solve the problems of justice and to facilitate an independent judicial power. Better collaboration is needed among all judicial personnel, because justice is the

---

[105] Ernélio Gassant is a licensed lawyer with the Bar of Port-au-Prince.

[106] Sabine Boucher, Magistrate, is graduate School of Judges.

[107] Renan Hédouville is lawyer and he is also the Secretary General of CARLI (Committee of Lawyers for the Respect of Individual Freedoms).

foundation of any modern and democratic society. Without healthy, equitable and impartial justice, there will be neither democracy, nor respect for human rights, nor sustainable development in Haiti.

Stanley Gaston[108]

The practices of the Haitian justice system, when considered as a whole, are very far from acceptable. The system's entire structure must be reformed, and its values redefined. Pragmatically and realistically, it amounts to recommending revolution. In my opinion, no partial reform will provide the desired result. What should be especially deplored is that the concepts of law and justice have been so dishonored that only those individuals whose moral values have undergone the most extraordinary decline benefit from the system.

Jean Vandal[109]

Justice in Haiti is dysfunctional. The great majority of Haitian judges are not up to the task. They are inexperienced. They lack knowledge of people and things. Young magistrates staff the district courts. These magistrates seek only promotions. Justice becomes fragile as a result. In addition, their basic needs aren't being met, from whence comes the plague of corruption within the system.

The penal level is a disaster. Magistrates pretend that sessions held at the National Penitentiary are public. Justice is removed from the local level by scattering courts around the country. Public prosecutor's offices are annexed in some communes like in Arcahaie.

The public prosecutor's office has an overabundance of deputies who do nothing and likewise, the outcome is the same for

---

[108] Stanley Gaston, lawyer, is the President of the Union of Young Haitian Lawyers.

[109] Jean Vandal is a former Minister of Justice and currently a licensed lawyer with the Bar of Port-au-Prince.

the overwhelming number of people in preventive detention. The work product of Investigative Judges leaves much to be desired. Major trials are not properly handled. We are far from the days of the great judges like Etzer Vilaire, Adrien Douyon, Rodolphe Bareau, Ireck Chatelain, Ismard Raymond, and Felix Kavanagh etc. The only defendants these days are simple, unknown individuals who are accused and then jailed indefinitely. The situation is not without remedy, but I am very pessimistic.

Gerard Gourgue[110]

A valid, objective and independent opinion of the current state of Haitian justice that takes into consideration its operations, its responsibilities and its independence with respect to the executive power, requires pulling together all the salient issues to a arrive at calm analysis of the question.

From the point of view of my personal experience of the actual position of things, is it not necessary to exclaim to the heavens as did Cicero: "Oh the times! Oh the morals!"

Given the climate of moral deterioration and decomposition into which the Haitian state devolved shortly after February 7, 1986, the present state of justice is the result of harmful and devastating effects that marked a long and painful transition that seems to have no end. For 46 years, there were judges in Berlin such as Dean Leon Pierre, a government prosecutor like Grévy Jean, outstanding judges like Solomon Kavanagh, and so on.

In those days, the executive had at least some decency not to interfere in grotesque and inopportune ways with court orders. Justice enjoyed a certain independence. This is not the reality we know today. Haitian justice became racketeer justice that guarantees only great injustice and social inequality throughout the country.

Camille Leblanc[111]

---

[110] Gerard Gourgue is a former Minister of Justice and former Bar Association president for lawyers of the Bar of Port-au-Prince.

Regarding the current operation of Haitian justice, the system has lost all the assets it possessed at the time I was Minister of Justice in the year 2000. My modernization campaign built on a three-point action plan was soon forgotten and the executive moved quickly to intensify its control over the judiciary. The three-point action plan consisted of:

1) De-politicization of the system;
2) Modernization of judicial tools;
3) Improved conditions for the distribution of justice.

Losing its independence, the judicial apparatus became more politicized each day. As an example, through the Ministry of Justice, the current executive power has created a small core of better-paid judges inside the district court of Port-au-Prince who aren't required to do anything. These judges, with the aim of protecting their petty interests, render decisions not in terms of the law or their consciences but according to the dictates of the executive power, thus causing two serious reactions in the collective conscience:

- Rejection of these magistrates by the population and by legal professionals who reproach them for their partiality.
- The fact that one feels the law is not in the process of being applied engenders an attitude of suspicion among the public and does not inspire any confidence in the distribution of justice. "They are political judges", one hears in the corridors of the palace of justice, not professionals who judge fairly.

The result: instead of leaving politics behind, the hand of the executive is strengthened over the judiciary.

Nothing was done to modernize the judiciary's equipment

The Ministry of Justice did take up certain projects that it then proposed to the legislature, but one has the impression that Parliament understood neither the meaning nor the means suggested.

---

[111] Camille Leblanc is a former Minister of Justice and currently a licensed lawyer with the Bar of Port-au-Prince.

The School for Magistrates created to train judicial staff closed its training program approximately three years ago. The commission charged with the reform of codes made no progress...

Justice for all: international cooperation efforts are neither concerned with nor encouraged to help in the field of legal aid.

Regarding creation of the means for better distribution of justice, we note that the old budget proposed nothing. We impatiently await the proposals of the new budget regarding the facts of innovation.

Meanwhile the same complaints are heard from Government Prosecutors, Justices of the Peace, Deans, examining magistrates and the Presidents of the Courts who report to the Ministry: no letterhead paper, no typewriters, no registers etc.

Conclusion: the judicial apparatus is treated as a poor relative and is sinking slowly into complete favoritism.

Henri Dorléans[112]

In 1995, Haiti had its best chance to begin true reform of its judicial system. Unfortunately, it seems only international donors truly desired such reform.

On the Haitian side: no reform plan, no political will, no dealing with international cooperation on the matter. Result: each donor defines its reforms and does its part with no governmental involvement; a lot of money is spent and no reform occurs.

We should not reform the judiciary for international donors. Reform is an absolute imperative today if one wants to promote the Rule of Law and the country's economic and social development. Let us cease holding conferences at the Montana Hotel, El Rancho or at the School for Magistrates, as if judicial reform consisted only of meetings and discussions, a nice lunch and quickly forgotten resolutions. Enough words! Time to act!

---

[112] Henri Dorléans is a university professor and former Minister of Justice. He is the author of the book: Judiciary Reform: a question of method and direction of responsibilities.

We have already let some very good opportunities pass by. But it is never too late to start. Judicial reform is like a baby. It is necessary to give it the care required for its growth and to keep from it what is harmful. The rest comes by itself.

Jean Marie Robert Paulvin[113]

An adequate understanding of the problems of Haitian justice is impossible without distinguishing between the inadequacy of the structures put in place by the State, and the slowness of justice that results from the administration of the judiciary.

Twenty-five years ago justice was adequately administered, to a certain extent. But lately, the time allotted for judgments according to international conventions ratified by Haiti is not respected. The same is true for all matters.

The problem of slowness is one of the bigger challenges to be solved in the Haitian judicial system. We find ourselves at the beginning of the 21st century. The existing infrastructure of the District Court of Port-au-Prince, for example, cannot process all of the defendants in the western department. This remark is true for all courts in all departments.

Any attempt to reform Haitian justice with the objective of making it more effective is destined in advance to failure if the infrastructure of the distribution of justice is not adapted to increasing demands.

Andre Michelle Civil[114]

Whenever one speaks of the judiciary, one looks at the functioning of the courts. In Haiti, courts intended to deliver justice confront all kinds of problems. On the one hand, the number of jurisdictions at every level of the judicial hierarchy is insufficient to meet society's needs; on the other hand, the individuals responsible for its operation lack sufficient expertise.

---

[113] Jean Marie Robert Paulvin is a licensed lawyer with the Bar Port-au-Prince.

[114] André Michelle Civil is a licensed lawyer with the Bar of Port-with Prince.

Moreover, the principles that govern various trial stages are for the most part out of date.

Faced with these difficulties, the persons in charge of the State need to adopt new regulations to normalize the entire judicial system.

Ketsia Charles[115]

The judicial system in Haiti is dysfunctional. Being a judge is no longer a noble profession. The media does nothing but degrade the image of the judiciary, and the authorities lack the will to place justice back on its pedestal.

Will the executive agree to divorce itself from the old tradition of exerting control over the judiciary, and in particular, over nomination to the judiciary? Will it really agree to grant the judiciary its independence?

Will there be the statutory conditions for judicial independence?

Statutory conditions for judicial independence also refers to the principles that govern judicial criteria: conditions for nomination, expertise and stability in the exercise of the judicial role. My wish for Haiti's judiciary is that it be able to recover from all these troubles. May the accused have confidence in its justice.

Antoine O. Vilaire[116]

The political and social upheavals long known in Haiti have greatly weakened the country's traditional institutions. Indisputably, the judicial institution has been most deeply affected, and reform is clearly inevitable in this field. One cannot claim to reform justice simply by enacting more sophisticated laws to govern its operation. One needs to focus on providing adequate human resources to respond effectively to the demands of a new

---

[115] Ketsia Charles, Magistrate, is a graduate of the School of Judges.

[116] Antoine O. Vilaire is a licensed lawyer with the Bar of Port-au-Prince.

judicial orientation to arrive at a rational vision that incorporates Haiti's social realities.

In-depth judicial reorganization requires completely reevaluating a judicial system that has for too long been stuck at the practical level.

1. Regarding magistrates and judicial personnel:

- Consider fixed terms of office for Justices of the Peace.
- Devise a law for judges and judicial personnel that offers certain guarantees, such as, career stability and mobility (personal safety, remuneration, conditions of service, systems of promotion etc.).
- Modify the decree of August 22, 1995 on judicial organization in order to guarantee the independence, objectivity, impartiality and stability of members of the judiciary.
- Equip the School for Magistrates, created by the Haitian constitution (Article 176), with a statute guaranteeing its role in judicial recruitment and promotion.

2. - Regarding penal legislation

- Abolish prison terms for all cases involving minor offenses
- Reconsider the principle of provisional release by proposing alternatives (such as the practice of granting bail)
- Simplify and modernize legal texts (formulation, language)
- Promulgate all laws currently in force, including common law, in Creole and in French in community councils, other local groups, municipal councils, schools, churches and universities to ensure viable justice in Haiti.
- Judiciously monitor the flow of orders to appear and orders of arrest.

N.B. According to the principle that freedom is the norm and imprisonment the exception, a well-known individual with a fixed address who is accused of something that is not a blood crime should have the benefit of the opportunity for conditional release upon deposit of a sum of money while his case follows its course to   the   investigative   judge.

Heidi Fortuné[117]

When one speaks of the dysfunction of the Haitian judicial system everyone points the finger at magistrates. Justice is a coherent system composed of various elements, *inter alia*: judges, government prosecutors, lawyers, clerks, bailiffs, police officers, experts and support staff. The judiciary is but one of its components, even if it is the most important. Elsewhere, in large countries, the Minister of Justice and the president of the Supreme Court have authority over the judiciary. But, here at home, the judiciary is dedicated to itself.

Judges are asked to guarantee defendants' rights while they themselves have no guarantees; they lack the means to complete their mission. They are badly remunerated and possess no social or environmental security. It makes us laugh when human rights organizations say in their reports that judges are responsible for prison overpopulation and the cancer that corrodes the system. How can magistrates be responsible for an institution's poor functioning? Article 136 of the Constitution stipulates clearly that the "President of the Republic is responsible for the stability of [government] institutions and ensures the regular operation of public powers." Magistrates are treated like poor relatives compared to members of Parliament and with members of the executive branch. One has only to glance at the budget allocated to the judiciary. Among senators, deputies and government officials, things are calm … one hears no complaints from them. Times are hard, but not for everyone.

We cry long and loud that judges are responsible for the misfortunes of the judiciary. Who selects untrained Justices of the Peace and inefficient and corrupt government prosecutors? Who should reform the laws? Who is responsible for renovation of the courts, continuing education, judicial specialization, materials and

---

[117] Heidi Fortuné is Examining magistrate at Cap-Haïtien and legal correspondent with the newspaper Le Matin.

technology, and the School for Magistrates? Who is responsible for filling vacant posts? Who is responsible for magistrates taking public transportation home after criminal hearings? Halls of justice into which magistrates are stuffed are not computerized, electrified, or secured. Who is responsible for these irregularities? Who works out, proposes, discusses and votes on the budget of the Republic, and by implication that of the judiciary? We ask everyone concerned to answer these questions. If, after all this, people persist in believing that magistrates are responsible for the judiciary's misfortunes, there can be only one of two conclusions, either that they are weak-minded, or they are in bad faith. Magistrates should not be made scapegoats. The treatment inflicted on them does not honor the country. Occasional seminars organized by the Ministry of Justice and sponsored in the majority of cases by the international community will not solve the problems.

A properly functioning judiciary requires an adequate infrastructure and well-defined strategies. The question of reasonable wages is of paramount importance. The diatribes launched from all corners will not change the situation as long as judicial civil servants are not comfortable, do not enjoy independence, and do not enjoy an atmosphere of confidence, and of non-interference where they are safe from temptation and corruption. People are always ready to condemn the judiciary but they close their eyes to the causes of dysfunction. The government, human rights organizations, and the international community lose no time reflecting on the problems that confront judges in their daily lives. Our urgent cry is: Help them, and they will help Haiti. A society that does not respect its judges and that has no faith in its judicial system sows the seeds of self-destruction. If the judiciary is a profitable trade for some, for others, it is a noble and honorable profession. To earn respect and to continue to exist, the judiciary must be brought under control.

Haiti: Justice Reform and the Security Crisis

Latin American/ Caribbean Briefing N°14, International Crisis Group, 31 January 2007

Overview

Violent and organized crime threatens to overwhelm Haiti. The justice system is weak and dysfunctional, no match for the rising wave of kidnappings, drug and human trafficking, assaults and rapes. If the efforts of the last three years to establish the rule of law and a stable democracy are to bear fruit urgent action is needed. Above all the Haitian government must demonstrate genuine political will to master the problem. But the international community also has a major support role. The immediate need is to establish, staff and equip two special courts, one a domestic criminal chamber to handle major crimes, the other a hybrid Haitian/international tribunal to deal with cases of transnational, organized crime that the country cannot tackle on its own.

Crime has surged since courthouses and prisons were looted and many of them destroyed in the lead-up to former President Aristide's departure in March 2004. The judiciary is encumbered by incompetence and corruption, partly due to inadequate pay, infrastructure and logistical support. The legal code is antiquated, barely modified since Napoleon bequeathed it to the one-time French colony, judges are not independent, case management is poor, and indigent defendants rarely have counsel. The state is able to guarantee neither the security of its citizens nor the rights of defendants. When arrests are made, the system is virtually incapable of conducting trials. Prisons become more crowded, and street crime escalates daily, while court procedures move at a snail's pace. The results are prolonged pre-trial detention – some 96 per cent of the inmates of the National Penitentiary have not been tried – lack of due process and near total absence of public confidence in the criminal justice system.

In the optimistic days after the democratically elected Aristide returned from exile in 1994, donors poured more than $43 million into justice reform. By 2000, when Aristide was re-elected, they had withdrawn almost all such support because they were convinced the government lacked political will. Aid has begun to flow again since Aristide's ouster but the obstacles are the same. The UN Mission in Haiti (MINUSTAH) and the new Préval government want to build a new justice system but corruption remains pervasive, including within the police and the judiciary.

Organized crime has put down roots, and urban gangs have yet to be disbanded.

Haitians and internationals need to take a sober look at past failings and devise, fund and implement a comprehensive rule-of-law strategy. Police reform will not succeed without parallel court reform. Building a criminal justice system that is sustainable requires a dual track effort: short-term actions to cope with the current crime wave and longer-term institution building.

In the short term, i.e., in 2007, the government and parliament need to:

- Enact into law a code of ethics for judges and an independent judicial council to enforce its provisions against corrupt judges;

- Authorize a special serious crimes court chamber with a vetted corps of judges, prosecutors and defense counsel and permit plea-bargaining with appropriate oversight; and

- Provide witness protection and better pay for judges;

Donors and MINUSTAH should coordinate with the ministry of justice's national strategy and provide trainers and funding for infrastructure, witness protection, forensic capabilities and legal aid.

In the longer term, the government and parliament need to:

- Amend the constitution to establish a more rational and effective procedure for appointing higher-level judges;

- Modernize the code of criminal procedure, establish a permanent panel to review cases of lengthy pre-trial detention and expand the use of fast-track procedures for prosecution of relatively minor crimes; and

- Build civil society support for justice reform;

Donors and MINUSTAH should ensure their programs extend for at least five years and, together with the government and other members of the Caribbean Community and Common Market (Caricom), should create a hybrid court with Haitian and other judges and personnel from the region to try transnational crime cases.

Urgent Need for Haitian Judicial Reform

The following section contains quotes from Juan Gabriel Valdés[118], a Chilean Diplomat and special representative of the Secretary General of the UN for Haiti, the chief of the Mission of the United Nations for Stabilization in Haiti (MINUSTAH); and from Danielle Saada, a French magistrate and head of MINUSTAH's justice section.

Saturday May 13 and Sunday May 14, 2006 edition of Le Devoir (http://www.ledevoir.com/2006/05/13/)

At MINUSTAH, we are convinced that the principal actors in essential comprehensive reform of Haitian justice will be Haitians themselves. Civil society and the Haitian people must be the ones in charge of their country's judicial system. Already committed to process of police force reform, MINUSTAH is listening to the concerns expressed by the organizations in Haitian civil society such the Citizen Forum, which has already made a proposal for a pact for the reform of justice.

At the heart of the Haitian drama

Haitian NGOs have long denounced many problems and obstacles: a total lack of organization and of financial means, a lack of coordination between the multiple agents of justice, absence of legal aid for the most impoverished, constant interference from the executive power, exploitation of the judicial system by political adversaries, illegal procedures, abusive detentions, etc. These Haitian organizations believe that the priorities of their next government must be the reform of justice and establishment of the Rule of Law.

Sharing this analysis, we are also persuaded that at the heart of the Haitian drama is the recurring problem of the general degradation of judicial institutions, the common denominator of the endemic plagues from which Haiti suffers (insecurity, violence, crime, impunity, human rights violations, etc). In Haiti, most criminals benefit from almost total impunity while, innocent

---

[118] Juan Gabriel Valdés, Chilean Diplomat and special representative for Haiti of the General Secretary of UN. For this reason, he is the chief of the Mission of the Nations Linked for Stabilization in Haiti (MINUSTAH).

people and wrongly accused suspects stagnate in prisons in preventive detention.

From our exchanges with the Haitian community, following principles have emerged and must be respected:

- *Judicial authority with respect to political and economic powers*. Judges must be paid adequate wages and must have congenial work conditions, with a judicial budget sufficient for its operation, and sufficient to guarantee the independence of the judiciary.

- *Real co-operation between the police force and justice is necessary*. No legal proceeding is credible without proper investigation. Judicial reform and police reform must go hand in hand. No purpose is served by a robust investigation if the analysis of the facts and the evidence does not lead to a legitimate verdict. Likewise, an illegitimate verdict, in the absence of legitimately gathered evidence, is no more acceptable.

According to our discussions with experts and NGOs in Haiti, the most urgent reforms to consider are the following:

• Establish a reform commission charged with modernizing Haiti's codes and laws, some of which are two centuries old, obsolete, unsuited, and not in conformity either with international standards or with international conventions adopted and ratified by Haiti - and in particular to re-examine the replacing custodial sentences with alternative sentences (probation, deferment, community service).

• Restructure the School for Magistrates to make it effective and functional again and to allow magistrates to pursue continuing legal education after nomination by means of a competition. This would require introduction of a recruiting competition and the establishment of initial and continuous training courses.

• Fight corruption in the judicial system by creating a true judicial investigation unit that will monitor judges and ensure their certification.

• Create the post of Secretary of State for Human Rights within the Ministry of Justice to demonstrate the importance of a culture of human rights, a culture that is still lacking in Haiti.

• Promote access to justice by creating a program of free legal aid for impoverished Haitians utilizing each county court's bar association and by implementing a system of more convenient justice (itinerant Justices of the Peace).

• Create specialized tribunals to handle organized crime with judicial personnel trained for this purpose, and provided with the necessary protections, conscious of its task and delivering legitimate verdicts within the statutes of limitation. These specialized tribunals could be set up as pilot projects for a special 12-month period and would hopefully have a domino effect within other county court tribunals.

The fight against violence cannot be accomplished without fighting corruption. The fight against corruption will not be successful without help from the international anti-organized crime community. The task as hand is considerable and urgent.

Cooperation Is Required

Canada, the United States, France and the European Union made financial contributions to Haitian judicial reform. The international community must continue supporting this process. The United Nations can provide technical support. Accordingly, judicial personnel from the UN police force (UNPOL) could assist with inspection of the Haitian police force and with management of criminal cases by the Haitian judicial police (DCPJ) to help them to organize investigation files and to gather evidence leading to indictment of criminals and gangs.

MINUSTAH is ready to support any legitimate judicial reforms in Haiti within the mandate granted to it by the Security Council. The international community must act together in Haiti, in a coordinated and coherent manner. Haitian judicial reform is a priority for everyone. The hope and thirst for change expressed by Haitians at the ballot box must be reinforced. The extraordinary democratic leap taken by the Haitian people at the time of the presidential elections, through mobilization of the masses to express and insist upon the need for change, must have a future. This message from Haitians all classes must be heard. We must answer it. Now more than ever we must mobilize, as well as find the political and financial means, so that vital judicial reforms can be sustained.

Danielle Saada[119]

The Haitian judicial system is weak, deprived of the funds necessary for its operations and undermined by corruption. The absence of follow-through and legal procedures on the part of the police constitutes a major handicap in the proper functioning of the Haitian judiciary. In Haiti, the fundamental problem is that proper procedures are not followed. Police and judicial proceedings drag on forever. Abusive, preventive, and prolonged detentions, impunity, a lack of organization and of means, no coordination between the judicial personnel, no legal aid for the poor, traditional interference from the executive power in the business of the judiciary, and the use of judicial power for political aims: these are among the many evils that devastate the system and demonstrate the urgent need for Haitian judicial reform.

To rectify this situation, MINUSTAH reaffirms its commitment to furnish assistance and advice to Haitian authorities to help monitor, reorganize and to reinforce the justice system. In answer to the protests lodged by Haitian lawyers in reaction to the idea of introducing French-speaking magistrates into the Haitian judicial system, the head of the UN Mission's Justice Section has stated in clear terms that the mission is not intended as a substitute for Haitian authority, but rather to provide assistance.

The objective is to establish the Rule of Law in Haiti so that the law is respected by all and for all.

Jacques Edouard Alexis[120], former Haitian Prime Minister

My Government will pay special attention to the implementation of judicial reform, without which the Rule of Law will never come to be in Haiti. It will also give special attention to Civil Service reform to ensure proper administration of the Haitian state.

---

[119] Danielle Saada, French, woman Magistrate and section head Justice of the MINUSTAH. (Press conference of Thursday, 5 October 2006).

[120] Declaration of General Policy of former Haitian Prime Minister Jacques Edouard Alexis, on June 6, 2006.

... An effective police force makes sense only if the judicial system is able to adequately answer its needs. In fact, it is all the problems of the criminal justice system that are concerned. My government recommends an integrated approach Justice/Police to equip the country with a system able to guarantee the safety of the citizens, to fight effectively against smuggling, the drug traffickers and the criminal gangs. The police force must also ensure control of the borders and immigration, considerable challenges with a coastline as large as ours.

The Superior Council of the National Police Force of which I am the statutory President will be responsible for the entire program, Security and Justice, as well as management of support from MINUSTAH.

M. Louis Joinet[121]

The greatest violation of human rights for the vast majority of Haitian people is, as has been stressed, poverty. In addition, the serious, repeated and unpunished violations of civil and political rights, that are a source of insecurity, including at the judicial level, not only oppress individuals, but also discourage both Haitian and foreign companies from investing in Haiti, and even force some of them to leave. Certainly, one cannot establish the Rule of Law without a functioning judiciary. The Haitian government must show its commitment to justice by fighting resolutely against impunity and by helping the judiciary to fulfill its mission. It must support the agents of the future, i.e. magistrates, police officers, and civil servants. They have been completely crushed, marginalized, even exiled. They must be given strength and courage. Without a clear demonstration of such commitment, any co-operation - even "revived" – will lose all credibility.

---

[121] Mr. Louis Joinet is independent expert of the UN on technical collaboration and the situation of Human Rights in Haiti.

The Coordinating Committee of the Citizen's Forum For the Reform of Justice: Jean-Claude Bajeux[122] - Jean Lhérisson[123]- Father Jan Hanssens[124]

Justice reform is above all reform of the State and its practices. It is not merely technocratic and technical reform. Justice reform consists of social and political reform that all of Haitian society demands, but which cannot hurried. To carry out such reform, the State authorities each have a specific role to play, for the duration of their terms in office, in ensuring respect for the proper rhythm of democracy. Moreover, citizen participation must not be circumvented, if one wants socially accepted reform. This participation must be included:

• At the time of the definition of the country's objectives in the field of justice.
• During establishment of State procedures (citizens and public authorities) to carry out the country's objectives.
• During the development of laws to establish the objectives and processes of judicial policy.

As the very principle of rational, effective and legitimate reform, it is essential that public authorities and civil society define the mechanisms for participation in the development of judicial policy:

- Communication between the State and organized civil society, including political parties, will allow democratization of debates. Inclusion of citizens is essential for the very legitimacy, rationality and effectiveness of justice reform.

- Accessible, transparent, precise and objective information allows for equal and rational participation of the agents of political dialogue: all agents must inform the others of their proposals, and actions.

- A clear, public reform agenda is essential to ensure communication and participation.

---

[122] Jean-Claude Bajeux is the director of the Ecumenical Center of Human Rights.

[123] Jean Lhérisson is the director of the International Haitian Solidarity Center.

[124] Père Jan Hanssens is the president of the Bishops' Commission for Justice and Peace.

THIRST FOR JUSTICE: WHERE IS JUSTICE REFORM?

Peace Brigades International - Haiti (Bulletin N0 9 March, 1998)

The demand for justice has always been one of the fundamental demands of the Haitian people, whether from civic and peasant groups, intellectuals, etc.

Haitian citizens proclaim their pressing desire for the establishment of the Rule of Law essential to a well-ordered society and to civic peace. This Rule of Law cannot be built on impunity, but must necessarily rest on the people's confidence in the legitimacy of democratic institutions, and in particular, of justice.

Has the Haitian democratic state made any progress, put into place any structures, passed any laws or committed to any reforms? Where is "the advent in Haiti of a qualitative, modern, effective, equitable and democratic justice system, a genuine social and economic regulatory instrument at the service of the entire population" as called for by former Minister of Justice Max Antoine?[125]

Justice in Crisis

According to Attorney Jean Sénat Fleury, magistrate and instructor at the National School For Magistrates, the report is bitter: "Haitian justice is in crisis, and its image with defendants has degraded with the passage of time. 95% of Haitians have no confidence in the justice system. The effects of judicial disengagement in Haiti are increasingly felt today in the form of a veritable explosion of unpunished infractions: theft, murder, assassination, and unjust enrichment... Forced to tolerate injustice, we have become in the end a society where virtually no law exists." This same assessment is repeated by the media as well as by civic and professional organizations.

---

[125] Max Antoine is a former Minister of Justice,1997.

According to a controversial report from the Ministry of Justice: "Haitian justice is decried because it is inaccessible to the masses due to its lack of organization, its poor performance, and its cost. The machinery of the police and the judiciary, as a system, seems to turn against the people (...) Haitian justice is characterized by its systemic inefficiency as much as by the problem of impunity, the latter of which seems to have become inherent in the system. The doctrine of national reconciliation negates justice and establishes impunity as a duty and a virtue."

An Unprecedented Development Effort

Since the return to constitutional order, new structures have been put in place. The Ministry of Justice has become one of the most important governmental institutions, a new police force and a School for Magistrates have been created, and the Prison Administration was reorganized.

International cooperation contributed significantly to these efforts. In 1997, fourteen new courthouses were inaugurated across the country, equipped with adjunct civil courts, thanks to the assistance of the Canadian government that supplied the necessary office equipment. Courts of Peace now function in locations hitherto deprived of them. With the creation of the Office of Citizen Protection, inaugurated last November 4 (which has already received many complaints), Haitians now have recourse for the Administration's abuses.[126] Lastly, the Ministry began nominating new officers for the Registry Office in order to apply the decree issued by former President Aristide concerning exemption from payment for all official documentation.[127]

---

[126] Article 207 of the Constitution of March 29, 1987 creates an office of the Protection of the Citizen whose goal is to protect all individuals against all forms of abuse by the public administration. A citizen who carries the title of Guard of the Citizen directs the Office. He is chosen by consensus between the President of the Republic, the President of the Senate and the President of the House of Commons. He is given a seven years mandate, nonrenewable. A decree of September 12, 1995 defines the organization, attributions and the operation of the Office.

[127] The decree of 1995 on the exemption from payment for the acts of civil status failed to generate an unblocking of all the system. The text had envisaged the

Ambitions of an Awaited Reform

The governmental commission that worked on the Reform of Law and Justice submitted a report to the Minister of Justice last December 10. The report, which was supposed to be distributed for comment and review to all concerned organizations, so far has remained confidential.

According to Florence Elie, president of the Commission (also in charge of the Raboteau lawsuit): "It really amounts to an autopsy of society's problems... The reform consists of a new approach to justice that took into account existing infrastructure and the relationship among the Executive, the Legislative and the Judicial branches to implement a coherent, complete and exhaustive reform methodology. Ours is a dual action plan: first, a five-year cycle, and then a second cycle of the same duration to consolidate what we have learned..."[128]

The Minister laid down the objectives of the reform project in 1996: "Judicial reform must seek to enable bringing together

---

free delivery of provision of birth certificates. However, it turns out that during the publication of this decree, not only did there not exist any registers - since the State had not provided any for a long time - but also even the forms for sending out, sold by the Bureau of Taxes, were not available. The decree of 1995 remained a dead letter.

[128] The Preparatory Commission for the Reform of Law and Justice (CPRDJ) (1997-1999) produced several working papers, one document of general policy, a strategic plan and a program for short-term actions. The Document of General Policy of the CPRJ does the analysis of the context of judiciary reform and the requirements of civil society with regard to the administration of justice, and proposes a new model of justice and a strategy of intervention.

The conclusions of the work of the Commission not only were ratified officially but the Government Plan of Action (PAG) of May 1999 specifically envisaged, as a priority, and with the title of social justice: "The enhancement, after validation, of the process of application of the Commission Proposals of Reform of the Law and Justice. " This declaration makes it possible to be based on an identification of needs officially expressed within the framework of overall policy. It is thus beginning with the "Document of General Policy" established as of July 1998, and with the Strategic Plan, which results in making it possible to take hold of the official priorities to try to respond to them within the framework of a long-term strategy of international assistance.

citizens and the judiciary. Consequently, the persons in charge of reform have a duty to explore all means of bringing justice closer to defendants, and to find new forms of participation."

During deliberations and preliminary research for the report regarding the structure of reform, modernization of institutions, independence of the judicial power, and continuous training of magistrates and auxiliaries of justice within the School for Magistrates were among the means emphasized.

In parallel, the report proposed rewriting Haitian codes and laws in Haiti's two official languages (French and Creole) the establishment of free legal assistance for the most impoverished so that they can be represented in court, and the dissemination of legal information in Creole.

Development of extra-judicial dispute resolution methods (arbitration, mediation), increasing the number of Judges and government prosecutors, and establishment of a Code of Ethics for judicial personnel are also recommended.

Lastly, the role of the national police force in its function as the auxiliary of the judiciary must be specified and formalized.

According to Max Antoine, the "action plan ... will be able to satisfy the major aspirations of the Haitian people for whom the combination of Rights and Justice means social peace, security for property and for people, respect for rights and freedoms, and economic prosperity."

The stakes are high, and 1997 ended with elegant declarations instead of concrete advances toward establishing a new, fair and democratic justice.

Contradictory Practices

On December 18, 1997, the Senate adopted draft legislation on the Reform of Justice first filed in Parliament on October 3 1996.[129]

---

[129] On December 18, 1997, the Senate adopted the framework legislation on the Reform of Justice filed in Parliament on October 3, 1996. The law became final in 1998. This law of May 8, 1998, published in the Monitor on August 17, 1998, concerning judiciary reform, puts at the very top of its objectives the reorganization of the Superior Council of Judges as the manager of judicial

The first article of the proposed law relates to the need for the judicial power's independence. Indeed, in Haiti, the judicial power has always been kept subordinate to the executive power. The Executive nominates, revokes and promotes magistrates at its discretion, in contradiction to the provisions of the 1987 Constitution. The draft article establishes (at least on paper) the separation of powers.

The second article relates to reorganization of the Superior Council of Magistrates, which had been quite ineffective in its mission "of offering magistrates the necessary guarantees of independence and impartiality." But, as judge Jean Sénat Fleury stated in an article published in Le Matin: "Is it enough to speak of reform, without mentioning political will? Will the Superior Council of Magistrates (CSM) assume its role in assisting the President with judicial nominations? Will the Executive respect the opinions of the CSM, made up of established, eminent personalities from throughout the judicial world ... ? Will disciplinary proceedings that lead to suspension be followed to the letter of the law...? The answers to those questions will demonstrate the limits of judicial reform based only on writing new laws without incorporating the political and social contexts

---

power and guarantor of the independence of the judges. This same element is taken up again among "the great choices" of the government Plan of action of May 1999, so obvious is the fact that the judiciary is currently suffering, in a formal and informal ways, the heavy and sometimes authoritative supervision by the executive.

The whole Napoleonic style judiciary organization is divided first of all into a hierarchical organization of jurisdictional levels. Thus the promotion of the subordinates depends on following a progressive concentration of power towards the top, of executive control.

- The power of the Minister of recall/nomination of Justices of the Peace has been maintained by the Constitution of 1987.
- Government prosecutors and their substitutes are the agents of executive power at the courts (Article 23 of the decree of August 25, 1995).
- The Justices of the Peace are the auxiliaries of the police courts and are thus in the orbit of their power.

- It is obvious that such a situation must be reconsidered if one wants to give independence to the judiciary.

that give rise to them. Judicial reform requires not only mobilizing the means, but also modifying behaviors."

Need for Genuine Dialogue

The National Commission On Truth and Justice drew up a list of absolute priorities for the reform of judicial institutions, without which progress is impossible. It isolated in particular "establishment of a process of questioning the design, the organization and the operation of the judicial system, support for the participation of associations, public human rights education, and wide distribution of a mass market version of the overall judicial reform plan..." However, until now, the reform plan has been prepared primarily in isolation within the Ministry, with an influx of foreigners whose interests are not necessarily compatible with the goals of the Haitian people.[130] Most importantly, the

---

[130] The observation component attached to an international mission could possibly lead to a series of perverse effects capable of resulting in the opposite effects envisioned and even of compromising local relationships. Indeed, if caution is not taken in this regard, the presence of a Mission is likely to reinforce the mentality of dependent stances and to anchor in the collective imagination the model of the foreign policeman.

Certain inertia of the administrative machinery can consequently tend to force the members of the Mission to end up becoming a replacement.

Far from producing positive effects, such an attitude can only contribute to defeatism, the displacement of responsibilities and to constituting an obstacle to the dynamics of exerting pressure on the State to help it to fulfill its functions fully.

If it is necessary to make a detailed study about the problems of justice in Haiti, it is necessary to call for in the very first place for national authorities (lawyers, sociologists, anthropologists, militants for human rights etc) who, surrounded by foreign authorities, can better make understood the problem arising from the coexistence of the two systems of law in Haiti: "a formal law and an informal law" which is seldom raised even in the current context marked by a desire for reform. Reform conceived by the liberal party of the elite, which has difficulty thinking of this other reality differently other than in an anecdotal way. However often, the differences between the two are marked.

To briefly suggest the importance of these differences I will quote these few lines of the anthropologist Andre Marcel d' Ans (1987) in connection with the land questions in Haiti: "The coexistence of two methods of owning property reveals in fact—just as it was the case in the Middle Ages - a state of tension between two concepts resting on antagonistic principles:

- On the one hand, under a "modern" system of property where the individual is subject to the law sui juris, land essentially has become a commodity of exchange. In this system, formalized by the Civil code, "no one required to remain in joint possession."

- And on the other hand, a system of inheritance where rights to land create membership in a "family company" for which land, representing the concrete element of social cohesion, is by definition inalienable."

Faced with the strong and authoritarian law of the elite being based on the Napoleonic codes, the other side has thus set up its own rules and its own solutions within the framework of practices which, although not codified, do not constitute any less of a true common or informal law, parallel with the official code which has always ignored them. At the beginning, as noted in a surprising enough way by one of the great Haitian lawyers of the 19th Century, Linstant Pradines: "In 1825 the Napoleonic code was adopted, with the political modifications that establish our customs and our institutions, modifications actually that are very few."

Apparently, as regards inheritance, of matrimonial status, family law and land law, the gap becomes more important and has not ceased widening since there has come about, for example regarding marriage, a special marital status, known as common-law, which is the status of more than 65% of the couples at the present time in the shantytowns and the countryside. As Me Exumé notes, former Minister for justice in 1995, there exists indeed in Haiti: "an informal law which can be more powerful than the formal law."

It would be difficult for the foreign expert to understand how social regulation in Haiti is still being carried out in practice. The weight that sorcery carries, the self administered-justice in the everyday life of the peasants, and even in the daily life of certain townsmen, this is what can be called popular justice or "a justice for the poor man".

A Haitian specialist Emerson Douyon, psychiatrist of Laval University Quebec), thus described this mechanism in 1984: "in addition, there exists a parallel or popular justice, reminiscent of certain places, usual customary African law. Expeditious justice, without appeal, subject to the law of retaliation, in conformity with the model of persecution... Attack and defense, magic and counter magic, are part of this model of mistrust and of persecution omnipresent in the system of magic. "To undo" for another customer what the preceding customer had asked you "to do", goes back to the need to always strengthen the "guard" for maximum protection. To play the two scenes at the same time, to work for the offense or defense in alternative ways, is part of the rules of the game of consultation in the relationship between the customer and his witch doctor. " Thus the problems of the reform of justice in Haiti are centered around

reform plan is being prepared without real participation and deliberation from all stakeholders in the Haitian judicial arena, as well without the participation of civic organizations and other interested parties.[131]

Thirst for Justice

It is undoubtedly still too early to assess the reforms now underway. What is obvious is that the Haitian people's thirst for justice remains unquenched. Many people continue to believe that true reform cannot be accomplished without a comprehensive approach that takes into account the demands of the entire Haitian people and that has the support of all of civil society.

At a time when a trial date for the Raboteau massacre has not yet been set (the facts date from April 1994), human rights and defenders of victims of the coup d'etat more than ever are

---

this extreme question, namely: " How to reconcile these two types of law, formal law and informal law in Haiti"?

It remains understood that the answer to such a question cannot be found except with the support of a State which carries out strategic choices and tactics and which integrates international assistance in its strategy of implementing of national policy. It follows from there that the projects must be conceived, set up and evaluated in the very first place with the local social and institutional agents and not with a surge of foreign helpers whose interests are not necessarily compatible with the aims sought after by the Haitian State.

[131] Too often the attempts at reform are taken up only as an offer of service that the State proposes. This unilateral and exclusive approach which leaves the examination of the constraints related to just the functioning of the judiciary institution does not take into account the citizens as actors of justice. So, justice has always remained an exclusive business of the State. However, it can be renewed only if it starts by recognizing the existence of forces within civil society with which to join to conclude the reform process. True decentralization, whose justice can become an example, rests, for example, on taking into account the initiative of such social actors. This function is normally reserved for a National Commission of Reform of Justice, which for better control of the whole of reform must be able to constitute the place of dialogue between the various actors concerned. This process not only allows recognition of the existence and the role of the various actors in justice but especially to make the style of the development of the code and law an exemplary process of the renewal of the democratic game.

mobilized to claim a real, equitable and democratic justice."[132] Whether in Gonaïves, the city of Independence, or in the capital,

---

[132] On April 22, 1994, three years after the coup d'etat which overthrew president Jean Bertrand Aristide, the Haitian army and paramilitaries of FRAPH (Front for the Advance and the Progress of Haiti) surrounded the district of Raboteau in Gonaïves in the North of Haiti.

During what is called now the Raboteau massacre, soldiers and forces of the FRAPH plundered the houses and shot at the inhabitants who tried to flee. They beat and tortured hundreds of people, pursued those seeking assistance at hospitals right up to Port-au-Prince. Whereas the death of only 8 people was documented, it is estimated that this day, there could have been more than fifteen people killed, but one will never know exactly the full number. The army prohibited the victims' families from coming to recover the bodies, which then quickly were burned or buried by the soldiers, devoured by pigs or dogs or carried away, by the sea.

The documentary Pote Mak Sonje (Creole: Keep the memory of your injury alive) presents the manner with which a community mobilized itself to lead to the capital trial of Raboteau. Told by certain survivors of the massacre of Raboteau, Pal Mak Sonje: the trial of Raboteau portrays their testimony charged with emotions of the key moments of this lawsuit. (Documentary completed in February, 2003, Harriet Hirston Productions).

Several soldiers confined in Gonaïves at the time of judging the facts were declared guilty, were condemned by the criminal court in session with the assistance of jury. All members of the High-State Major army of Haiti in flight were judged and condemned in absentia. But, the Supreme Court in a stay of May 3, 2005 overturned the judgment returned on November 10, 2000 by the Criminal Court of Gonaïves with the reason that this latter, "sitting with assistance of the jury rationae materiae (by reason of the matter) was incompetent to recognize the crimes and offences alleged against the defendants."

According to the arguments advanced by the Supreme Court on May 3, 2005, the Criminal Court of Gonaïves, in session with assistance of a jury, was not qualified to judge the affair, which renders the decision null and void. The Supreme Court cited the support of the law of March 29, 1928. [Art 3 of the law of March 29, 1928: In interconnected cases envisaged in article 110 of the criminal instruction code, as well as whenever the infringements would have been done by the same individual, if one of them is qualified as a crime, the investigative judge ruling on the whole by only one decision will bring the cause back in front of the criminal court which will judge without the assistance of the jury].

Amnesty International considers that the arguments presented by the Supreme Court to justify the cancellation of the penalties are contrary to the Haitian Constitution and that the Supreme Court, by basing its decision on the law of March 29, 1928, denies the primacy of the Constitution. In his report presented on January 9, 2006 before the Commission of Human rights (sixty-second session - Point 19 of the provisional order day), the independent expert of the United Nations for Haiti, Louis Joinet criticized the decision in his terms: "According to article 50 of the Constitution, "the jury is established for criminal matters for the crimes of blood." The investigative chamber thus returned at that time a dismissal order to the criminal court sitting "with jury", validated by the Court of Appeal and then - this point is important - with a stay of the Supreme Court having become finalized, rendered at the time "on the agreed upon conclusions" of the Police chief close to the Boniface Alexandre Court having become thereafter President of the Supreme Court and current provisional President of the Republic.

But served in 2005 with a new appeal, the Supreme court - contradicting the Constitution by not explaining "what it is necessary to understand by crime of blood" (sic), these top judges should have applied the law of 1928 (however prior to the Constitution!) which stipulates that, except in the cases of murder, parricide or imprisonment, if there exist related infringements, the judgment must be returned "without jury". (It should be noted that related infringements had been retained however in the first arrest!) Such is the reasoning which led the Court to consider that these criminals, having been condemned at the time without hesitation – be given a reverse judgment. Reason: by an incompetent court, their release was essential immediately.

It will have been understood that the first stay validating competence "with jury", in addition to the fact that it was respectful of the Constitution, had acquired the authority of "res judicata" since it was about the same affair, implicating the same people, for the same facts of comparable nature, related infringements with the same time and place and that, the grounds for appeal having been exhausted at the time, the order was final.

" N.B. Charged with investigating all the files having been the object of great publicity, I had this privilege as examining magistrate to carry out the investigation or in particular to pose acts about several cases usually called "sensitive files" in Haiti: the Raboteau Affair, files of Jean Léopold Dominique, Jean-Marie Vincent, Piâtre, of Mireille Durocher Bertin, Gerard Jean Right, toxic waste in Gonaïves, cases of drug etc

But too occupied at the time by the large number of cases to handle - more than two hundred cases listed sometimes in the register, - I could realize with difficulty at that time that all the work of investigation achieved at the price of hard sacrifices, of humiliations, with danger even to my person and my family was wiped out. The Haitian judiciary apparatus as a monster devoured all my orders.

See the Reverse Order rendered by the Supreme Court of Port-au-Prince in the case of the assassination of father Jean Marie Vincent.

"The Reverse Orders of the Supreme Court of Port-au-Prince on the related case of the assassination of Father Jean-Marie Vincent constitutes an additional proof of the incapacity of the judiciary apparatus to answer the demands for justice of

the denunciations of human rights abuses continue. Every Wednesday, from 11 a.m. to noon, dozens of people march to obtain reparations, inspired by the Argentinean movement of the Mothers of Plaza de Mayo. Various organizations continue to call for the return of files of the FRAPH, seized by United States armed forces in 1994.

At the same time, Justices of the Peace and government prosecutors go on strike to draw the attention of government authorities to the failures of the judiciary. "The judiciary", writes Atty. Fleury, "figurehead of the new Haitian democracy, is in crisis. The symptoms of the crisis are well known: arbitrary suspensions, absence of judicial independence, mistreatment, absurd salaries..." These Magistrates denounce the fact that the police force, considered as an auxiliary to justice, is better equipped and better paid. Often regarded as corrupted flimflam artists, judges have ended their silence and have denounced the constraints and difficulties of their profession. "The more justice functions poorly, the more it is used as scapegoat." (Chronicles of Jean Sénat Fleury in Le Matin Nov. 97).

Will the year 1998 see the advent of an equitable and democratic justice demanded by Haitian society? Will it see the end of impunity and the introduction of a genuine Rule of Law?

---

the Haitian people. It constitutes an eloquent testimony to the lack of seriousness that characterizes the treatment of the criminal files at the level of justice. The system shows clearly for everyone to see its inefficiency and its efficiency.

Judge Jean Sénat Fleury's Order remanding to the Criminal court, with the assistance of a jury, eleven (11) supposed assassins (authors, silent partners, and accomplices) of Jean-Marie Vincent was overturned because the Clerk of the investigating judge did not sign the order. Why did he not sign? Was it by negligence or a deliberate act? No one will ever know. But nine (9) years of investigations carried out by four (4) investigative judges are reduced to nothing by the lone fact that the Clerk did not sign the order of closure. What Justice?

Report of the National Network of the Defense of Human rights - RNDDH, July 6, 2005.

Cries of increasing frustration, dissatisfaction and despair ring from all corners. Simultaneously, the political crisis commenced in June 1997 holds the entire country hostage, paralyzing the proper functioning of government institutions. In the meantime, duly sworn Haitian political officials must keep in mind that: "Justice for one, is Peace for all."

Claude Gilles, Le Nouvelliste, August 10, 2007

Justice Reform Submitted For Review By Parliament

Only human rights organizations, peasants, and laborers... complain about the Haitian judiciary's poor performance. Outmoded customs and practices that do not pay homage to the "togas" (robed ones) are pressuring the Préval/Alexis administration to submit judicial reform legislation for review by Parliament.

Senate ratification of two of the three pieces of legislation on Haitian justice reform made UN Secretary Ban Ki-Moon jubilant. "A great step toward judicial reform," the smiling General Secretary of the United Nations professed at President René Préval's side, when only seven years ago he proclaimed the Haitian judiciary to be "rotten." The vote - a seminal victory for the Préval/Alexis administration – gave Senator Youri Latortue confidence in the judicial reform process. "Since 1994 no law on Haitian justice reform has been passed by Parliament," the president of the Senate Justice and Safety Commission and Safety emphasized.

One of the two bills ratified by senators envisages the creation of the Superior Council of Magistrates, "the body of administration, discipline and deliberation of the [judicial] power." One of the Superior Council's primary missions is to issue opinions regarding judicial nominations and to review each magistrate's career advancement. The council, comprised of the president of the Courts of Appeal, the Supreme Court's Government Prosecutor, a Judge from the Court of Appeal, a representative of civil society and a president of an attorney's bar, shall supervise and disseminate information and make recommendations regarding the state of the judicial branch. If the House of Commons approves the bill, eight members of the Superior Council of Magistrates shall be named by presidential decree subject to review by the Minister of Justice and Public Safety.

Promoted by the coalition government of Jacques-Edouard Alexis these reforms envision the judicial power's economic independence that will "direct and manage the operational budget allocated to the Courts and Tribunals." For that to happen, the bill awaiting a vote by the House of Deputies proposes the installation of a technical secretariat "to manage the material and financial resources of the judicial power, to contribute to the development of the judicial power's draft budget, to carry out the judiciary's budgetary powers, and to sign checks..." The judiciary's starvation wages have long been identified as one of the causes of judicial corruption. Justices of the Peace in remote towns and the villages are the worst off. They must find the means to live on less than 200 American dollars a month. "It is not always easy to keep up with notorious locals, accustomed to making hay while the sun shines within illiterate populations," Syfia International notes. "After a while," the agency emphasizes, "many [judges] become dealmakers and require 'compensation; in order to undertake an investigation or to issue orders. According to article 22 of the bill, "any person believing him/herself to have been the victim of a magistrate's [unethical] behavior will be able to bring a claim before the Superior Council of Magistrates. A legitimate complaint with acknowledgement of delivery will be lodged with the Ministry for Justice and Public Safety by means of the Government Prosecutor within a time not exceeding seventy-two hours. The ministry", the document specifies, "transmits the complaint to the Superior Council of Magistrates and notifies the plaintiff of its receipt. If, after a delay of fifteen days after deposit of the complaint, the plaintiff has not received notification of this transmission, he can then address the Council directly."

"In the event of emergency and whatever mode of notification", article 34 of the bill indicates that "on recommendation of the Ministry for Justice and Public Safety, "the Superior Council of Magistrates can forbid a judge from performing his duties while he is the subject of ongoing disciplinary action until his case has been definitively decided." The Superior Council of Magistrates, according to legislation passed by the Senate, possesses a generalized power regarding any and all judicial issues, in particular, those concerning the independence of the judiciary and sound operating procedures.

THE AUTHOR

Born September 10, 1963, Jean Sénat Fleury is a graduate of the Faculty of Law and Economic Sciences in Port-Au-Prince. Trained at the National School for Magistrates in Paris and Bordeaux, he worked in different capacities within the Haitian judicial system, and as an instructor in the National Police Academy (1995). Trainer and director of studies at the School for Magistrates (2002) Jean Sénat Fleury worked for eighteen years as a judge in Haiti. As presiding judge he investigated the case of the Raboteau massacre in Gonaïves and investigated several important cases (assassination of the journalist Jean Dominique, of Father Jean-Marie Vincent, of Mireille Durocher Bertin, of accusations of the Boniface-Latortue government against Father Gérard Jean Juste, and he was the judge in charge of investigating drug cases. He is currently a practicing lawyer in the Bar of Port-Au-Prince.

"Independence of the judicial system is essential in a democracy. If those who hold political power can use it to settle judicial problems, then justice will not survive. From that moment on leaders will be able to arbitrarily impose their will on the judges, and dismiss them, and democracy will disappear completely, and then we become an outlaw state, a regime without law." Jean Sénat Fleury, "The Supreme Court And Judicial Reform In Haiti (Printer: Rivet P.E. – Limoges March 2006).

BIBLIOGRAPHY

1. *Actes du colloque international sur les Droits Humains en Haïti*, Port-au-Prince 1993.
2. Anvers, Paul. *Rivières de sang*. Paris : l'Harmattan, 1992.
3. Aristide, Jean-Bertrand. *Shalom 2004*, Imprimerie Henri Deschamps.
4. Aristide, Jean-Bertrand. *Tout Homme est un Homme*. Paris : Editions du Seuil, 1992.
5. Delince, Kern. *Armée et Politique en Haïti*, Paris : Editions l'Harmattan, 1979.
6. Barthélemy, Gérard. *Le pays en dehors, essai sur l'univers rural en Haïti*, 2e éd. Éditions Henri Deschamps, Port-au-Prince, 1989.
7. Bastien, Rémy. *Haitian Rural Family Organization*. Social and Economic Studies, 1961.
8. BID. *Plan d'opérations, Programme de modernisation du registre d'état civil* (HA 0083).
9. César Jumelle, Michelle. *La Réforme de la Justice Haïtienne - Doctrine* ; Revue Juridique de l'Université Quisqueya, volume II No 1, Port-au-Prince, Janvier-Juin 2000.
10. Civil, André. *Les parquets et les tribunaux en Haïti : problèmes et perspectives, mémoire de sortie*, mars 1999.
11. Communiqué de presse du Bureau de la coordination des affaires humanitaires 2004, sur www.reliefweb.int. Selon le PNUD, 50 p. cent de la population n'a pas accès à l'eau potable. Voir www.ht.undp.org/humanitaire.
12. COOPÉRATION FRANÇAISE. *Conciliation et arbitrage en Haïti*, mars 1999.
13. CPRDJ. *Document de politique générale*, juillet 1998.
14. CPRDJ. *Dossier de rapports des travaux de la CPRDJ*, juillet 1999.
15. Dejean, Paul. *Haïti : Alerte, On Tue*. Montréal : CIDIHCA, 1993.
16. Désir, Marie-Ange. *La problématique de la corruption en Haïti et les mesures légales*, mémoire pour le grade de licencié en droit, mai 2007.
17. Dieng, Adama. *Rapport sur la situation des Droits de l'Homme en Haïti*, avril 1999.
18. Dorléans, Henry. *La réforme judiciaire : une question de méthode et de sens de responsabilités*, oct. 2001.
19. Exumé, Jean Joseph. *Rapport d'observation préliminaire sur la situation de la justice en Haïti*, décembre 1996.
20. Forum National sur la Justice au Mali. *Mémoire du groupe de réflexion sur le thème : Justice et Corruption.*
21. HSI. *Les conclusions de la Commission Nationale Vérité et Justice – Recommandations.*
22. Jacques Edouard Alexis.

Déclaration de Politique Générale du Premier Ministre, juin 2006.

23. J.B. Roumain. *Quelques mœurs et coutumes des paysans haïtiens : Travaux pratiques d'ethnographie sur la région de Milot à l'usage des étudiants.* Port-au-Prince : Imprimerie de l'Etat, 1959.

24. Joachim, Benoît. *Les Racines du Sous-développement en Haïti.* Port-au-Prince : Henri Deschamps, 1979.

25. Kofi, Annan. "In Haïti for the long Haul", in Wall Street Journal, 16 mars 2004.

26. La Constitution d'Haïti du 29 mars 1987.

27. La loi sur la réforme judiciaire du 22 août 1995.

28. LeFeber, Walter. *Inevitable Revolutions.* New York : Norton, 1984.

29. Lemaire Lhérisson, Dilia. *La Justice en Haïti aujourd'hui.*

30. Loïc, Cadiet et Laurent, Richer. *Réforme de la Justice, Réforme de l'État,* Presses Universitaires de France, 2003.

31. Manigat, Mirlande. *Plaidoyer pour une nouvelle Constitution,* Port-au-Prince, Imprimerie Deschamps, 1995, Collection CHUDAC.

32. MANUH/MICIVIH. *Troisième diagnostic national sur la justice, la police et les prisons,* juillet 1997.

33. Mattarollo, Rodolfo. *Une plaidoirie pour l'application des traités internationaux relatifs aux Droits de l'Homme par les Tribunaux haïtiens,* avril 1998.

34. MICIVIH. *Le système judiciaire en Haïti, Analyse des aspects pénaux et de procédure pénale,* mai 1996.

35. MICIVIH, *Droit des mineurs et des femmes détenus,* Claudine Jacob, 1997.

36. Mills, C. Wright. *The Power Elite.* Oxford : Oxford University Press, 1956.

37. Ministère de la Justice et de la Sécurité Publique. *Regards sur l'Organisation Judiciaire en Haïti* 1995-1997.

38. Moïse, Claude and Emile Ollivier. *Repenser Haïti : Grandeur et Misères d'un Mouvement Démocratique.* Montréal : CIDIHCA, 1992.

39. Montalvo, Despeignes, Jacquelin. *Le droit informel haïtien,* PUF, Paris, 1976.

40. Neptune, Anglade Mireille. *L'autre Moitié du Développement : A Propos du Travail des Femmes en Haïti,* Édition des Alizes, 1986.

41. O'Nell, William. *The Roots of Human Rights Violations in Haïti.* Georgetown Immigration Law Journal, 1993.

42. Pierre, Jean Larrio. *De l'Indépendance Effective du Pouvoir Judiciaire en Haïti,* mémoire présenté pour l'obtention du grade de licencié en droit, avril 2006.

43. Pierre-Louis, Josué. *Haïti et ses institutions,* imprimerie Henry Deschamps, oct. 2005.

44. PNUD. *Atelier stratégie à long terme pour Haïti, Stratégie pour le secteur justice,* novembre 1997.

45. PNUD. Assistance à la Réforme Pénitentiaire – Phase II, Document de projet 36. (HAI/99/004).

46. PNUD. Situation Economique et Sociale d'Haïti en 2004, P-au-P août 2005.

47. POHDH et NCHR. *Pour un plan d'action contre l'impunité,* septembre 1998.

48. Précil, Privat. *Déportés et déplacés : un phénomène migratoire, un problème social,* The Panos Institute, mai 1999.

49. Programme des Nations Unies pour le Développement, Bureau pour l'Amérique Latine et les Caraïbes. *Justice en Haïti,* octobre 1999.

50. Reynand, Pierre. *État de Droit et les Tribunaux de Paix,* 1998.

51. Rivière, Roodley. *Les difficultés de la mise en œuvre du Recours pour la Protection de la liberté individuelle dans le droit haïtien,* mémoire présenté à l'Université Quisqueya pour le grade de licencié en droit, avril 2003.

52. Salvatore, Senese – Pierre-Charle, Gérard – Asbjorn, Eide – Texier, Philippe. *Droits Humains, Justice et Impunité,* éd. CRESFED, P-au-P, 1993, 39 pages.

53. Saint-Louis, Léon. *Rapport sur l'État du Pouvoir Judiciaire,* Editions des Antilles, avril 2004.

54. Sénat Fleury, Jean. *La Cour de Cassation Face à la Réforme Judiciaire en Haïti,* imprimerie Rivet Limoges – France, mars 2006.

55. Union Européenne. Rapport Mission Daniel de Beer : *La Justice,* décembre 1997.

56. Université Paris I, Centre de Droit International. *Aspects juridiques de la crise d'Haïti,* 1995.

57. USAID/Haïti. *Evaluation of USAID's Administration of Justice and Human Rights,* Juillet 1998.

58. USAID/Haïti, Louis Aucion, Jean Joseph Exumé, Ira Lowenthal, Harvey Rishikof. *Assessment of the Justice sector in Haiti,* November 1997.

59. Vieux, Serge Henri. *Le plaçage, droit coutumier et famille en Haïti,* Editions Publisud, Paris, 1989.

60. Vincent, Jean – Guinchard, Serge – Montagnier, Gabriel – Varinard, André. *La Justice et ses Institutions,* 4ème éd. Dalloz, Paris, mai 1966.

61. Vixamar, Jean-Philippe. *Problématique de la Réforme Judiciaire en Haïti,* mémoire présenté pour l'obtention du grade de licencié en droit, mars 1996.

INDEX

1987 Constitution, 14, 19, 48

access to justice, 17, 19, 54, 55, 56, 88, 104

access to rights, principle of, 57

accessibility, principle of judicial, 54

Alexis, Jacques Edouard, 45, 46, 71, 81, 83, 86, 106, 120, 123

anti-corruption watchdog group, 42

Antoine, Max, 109, 112

APENA, 67, 80

arbitrary detention, 79

Aristide, Jean-Bertrand, 8, 28, 38

Article 136, 1987 Constiuttion, 98

Article 174, 1987 Constitution, 31

Article 175, 1987 Constitution, 32

Article 177, 1987 Constitution, 32

Article 59, 1987 Constitution, 48

article 60, 1987 Constitution, 32

Assessment of the Justice Sector in Haiti, 13

AUMOHD, 5, 7, 8

Avril, Prosper, 30, 31

Bajeux, Jean-Claude, 89, 107

Bale Wouze, 29

Bareau, Rodolphe, 92

Boniface, Alexandre, 32

Boucher, Sabine, 90

Brown, Jean-Baptiste, 31

Butcher, Sabine, 89

Canadian Agency of International Development, 37

Charles, Ketsia, 89, 96

Chatelain, Ireck, 92

Citizen Forum, 102

Civil, Andre Michelle, 89, 95

common law, 9, 51, 56, 60, 70, 97

commune, 9, 54, 56, 68

Community Human Rights Council, 5, 7, 8

corruption, 12, 36, 38, 39, 40, 41, 42, 46, 61, 91

media campaign against, 43

strategies for eliminating, 41

Council of Europe, 36

Council of the Wise (Le Conseil Des Sages), 31

Court of Appeals, 23, 29, 33, 34

Courts of First Appeal, 24, 55

Courts of Peace, 23, 24, 25, 51, 62, 68, 110

courts, distribution of, 11

CPRDJ, 13, 61, 64, 111, 123

Creole, 10, 55, 97, 111, 117

DCPJ, 104

DDR – disarmament, demobilization, reinegration, 78

decree of August 22, 1995, 25, 26, 32, 50, 64, 68, 97

decree of June 5, 1995, 67

decree of March 29, 1979, 22, 58

decree of September 27, 1985, 67

Dieng, Adama, 13

disarmament plan, national, 72

Dorléans, Henri, 49, 89, 94

Douyon, Adrien, 92

Dubreuil, Jean Gerard, 30, 31

Duplan, Rigaud, 30, 31

Elie, Florence, 111

Ethics, Code of, 43, 66, 112

Exantus, Laraque, 5

execution, extrajudicial, 80

exemption from payment, principle of, 57

Fabien, Brédy, 29

Faculty of Law of the State University of Haiti, 49

fair trial, right to a, 57

Fleury, Jean Sénat, 2, 5, 6, 7, 29, 35, 36, 109, 113, 118, 119, 122, 125

Fortuné, Heidi, 89, 98

FRAPH, 116, 119

Friends of Lawyers, 30

Gassant, Enerlio, 89

Gassant, Ernélio, 90

Gaston, Stanley, 89, 91

Gourgue, Gerard, 89, 92

Gousse, Justice Minister Bernard, 29, 50

Government Prosecutor, 15, 24, 28, 121

Guillaume, Ramon, 29

Hanssens, Father John, 89, 107

Hédouville, Renan, 89, 90

hospitality, principle of judicial, 55

human rights, justice and, 7, 8, 12, 13, 18, 30, 40, 42, 53, 58, 62, 71, 75, 76, 77, 78, 79, 80, 81, 82, 84, 89, 91, 114

HURAH, 7, 8

incapacity, 31, 32, 50, 64, 118

Inter-American Commission on Human Rights, 19

Inter-American Convention Against Corruption, 37

Inter-American Development Bank, 10, 37

International Monetary Fund, 37

Investigative Judge, 24

Investigative Office, 24, 26

irremovability, 50

irremovability of judges, 50

itinerant judges, 55

Jean, Grévy, 92

job security, 16, 52, 72

Joinet, Louis, 13, 89, 106, 117

judicial independence, 14, 32, 34, 48, 50, 51, 72, 90, 96

criteria for reinforcing, 51

judicial inefficiency, 25

Judicial Investigation
    Department, 72
judicial reform
    comprehensive option for,
        47

    minimalist option for, 47
Judicial Reform
    Commission, 87
judicial reform,
    recommendations for, 61
Julien, René, 30
justice, great principles of, 57
Justices of the Peace, 23, 24,
    25, 32, 48, 53, 60, 94, 97,
    99, 112, 113, 119, 121
Kavanagh, Felix, 92
Latortue, 6, 8, 30, 31, 33, 78,
    120, 122
law of June 6, 1919, 67
lawlessness, 74
    factors contributing to, 74

    proposals for eliminating,
        75

Leblanc, Camille, 89, 93
Lebrun, Jean-Joseph, 29
legal aid, 57, 58, 59, 67
Legros, Gladys, 89
Lhérisson, Jean, 89, 107
magistrate, grand jury, 67
Magistrates, School for, 49,
    51, 66, 81, 88, 94, 95, 97,
    99, 104, 111
Magistrates, Superior
    Council of, 42, 51, 64,
    113, 120
Mayette, Amanus, 29

Mérida Convention. *See*
    United Nations
    Convention on Corruption
MICIVIH, 13, 53, 59, 124
Minister of Justice, 15, 28,
    29, 34, 35, 49, 91, 92, 93,
    94, 109, 110, 120
MINUSTAH, 12, 13, 46, 77,
    102, 105, 106
MIPONUH, 13
modernization, 86
Napoleonic Code, 9
National Commission On
    Truth and Justice, 13, 61,
    113
National Penitentiary, 8, 27,
    63, 80, 91
Nelson, Eddy, 89
Neptune, Yvon, 8
Noël, Henry Kesner, 30, 31
Organisation of American
    States, 31, 37
Organization of Cooperation
    and of Economic
    Development, 37
Paulvin, Jean Marie Robert,
    89, 95
Piâtre Massacre, 30
Pierre, Leon, 92
Police Ethics Commission,
    77
police reform, 75
political interference, 28,
    103
politics of the belly, 37
private justice, 11
Professional advancement,
    15
Prosecutor's Office, 23, 24,
    25, 67

Protection, Office of Citizen, 110
provisional release, principle of, 97
proxies, 22
Public Prosecutor, 23
public safety, 72, 77, 87
Public Service, National, 85
Radio Metropole, 30
RAMICOSM, 29
Raymond, Ismard, 92
Rule of Law, 14, 16, 17, 24, 30, 38, 41, 42, 56, 70, 71, 72, 77, 82, 84, 86, 89, 95, 103, 106, 107, 108, 119
Saada, Danielle, 89, 102, 105
Saint-Pierre, Hugues, 29
salaries, judicial, 52
satisfaction, principle of judicial, 56
Schoelcher, Victor, 10
Scierie Case, The, 28
separation of powers, 14, 33, 113
SIMEUS /CEP, 33

slow justice, 27
specialization, judicial, 49, 52, 53, 84, 99
Supreme Court, 6, 23, 31, 32, 33, 64, 66, 68, 98, 117, 118, 120, 122
Talion, La Loi du, 11
Termination of Five Judges, 31
training, 49
Transparency International, 37, 38
transparent inspection system, 43
UNDP, 11, 12, 13, 18, 20, 54
United Nations Convention Against Corruption, 38
UNPOL, 104
USAID, 13, 59, 125
Valdés, Juan Gabriel, 89, 102
Vandal, Jean, 89, 91
Vilaire, Antoine, 89, 96
Vilaire, Etzer, 92
World Bank, 36, 37